LONELY COMMAND

A. A. HOEHLING

LONELY COMMAND

A Documentary

With eight pages of half-tone illustrations

NEW YORK: THOMAS YOSELOFF, INC.

Set in 12 *pt. Bembo type and*
printed in Great Britain by
Wyman and Sons Ltd., London, Reading & Fakenham
F.557

ILLUSTRATIONS

ACKNOWLEDGEMENTS

I should like to express my thanks to all those who helped me by providing information during the writing of this book, and in particular Prince von Hohenzollern-Emden and Admiral Witthoeft-Emden. My thanks are due also to the *Atlantic Monthly* for allowing me to reproduce extracts from the diary of Signalman Seabrooke.

Finally I should like to thank the Exclusive News Agency, the Imperial War Museum, C. A. Ribiero & Co. Ltd., Singapore, and Qantas Airlines, for allowing me to reproduce certain of their photographs.

This is the story of a sea raider, the *Emden* . . . of its Captain, Karl von Müller, and of that loneliness of heart and soul which only those who have known command, and command by themselves can fully understand.

I am tired and sick of war. Its glory is all moonshine.
It is only those who have neither fired a shot nor heard
the shrieks and groans of the wounded who cry aloud
for blood, more vengeance, more desolation. War
is hell.

GENERAL WILLIAM T. SHERMAN,
*in 1879, before the graduating class
of the Michigan Military Academy*

CHAPTER I

THE November morning, by nine o'clock, had arrived with a broiling relentlessness. The sun glinted off the flat, blue surface of the Indian Ocean and was magnified in intensity a thousandfold. Even the querulous, swarming, men-o'-war birds lost a certain measure of their aggressiveness to the atmosphere's torpor.

Only the palm trees on tiny Direction Island held up their fronds, green and stiff, to the beating heat. This was the Indian Ocean. These were the Cocos Atolls, pin-pricks of coral lost in a sub-Equatorial wilderness of trackless sea, 1,600 miles north-west of Perth, 1,800 miles south-east of Ceylon. They were home to a handful of people, as well as to a cable and wireless station of the Eastern Extension Telegraph Company, part of London's complex of nerve fibres to a scattered and now threatened Empire.

It was this important relay station that had attracted Karl von Müller and his little *Emden*. This was the cynosure to which the forty-one-year-old captain and his complement of 320 officers and men had steamed from hunting grounds off the sparkling Sumatra coast.

The German cruiser no longer had even the solace of a home port, for Tsingtao, base of the Imperial Asiatic Squadron, had fallen several days ago. She was as scarred, dirty and barnacled from three months at sea as her men were weary and, deep in their hearts, homesick. She seemed a living refutation of her former nickname, 'Swan of the East'. Spit-and-polish had long since been forgotten; in addition to extra piles of coal bunkered in odd corners of the deck, even sheep and pigs tethered to ventilators and stanchions and haphazard crates of chickens stamped this warship as one existing desperately.

Blond, tall, quiet-mannered and above all thoughtful, Captain von Müller watched through powerful binoculars the progress of his raiding party ashore. His first officer, Hellmuth von Muecke, had landed after daybreak with fifty men. Their destruction of Direction Island's transmitters was now well under way. Von Müller had seen the radio mast topple, accompanied by a white puff of smoke at its base.

His cruiser was riding easily at anchor, so peacefully under the tropical sun that there was almost foreboding in the very calm. Port Refuge, so-called, was a poor enough shelter: simply a shallows, the wide coral horseshoe of the low-lying Cocos (or Keelings) group. Within the 3,200-ton cruiser's vitals the generators hummed and the furnaces glowed with their pungent burden of coal . . . always, always in readiness to leap forward to defend herself.

As von Müller was well aware, *Emden* had led a hunted existence. Only a week ago he had counted at least sixteen capital warships of five navies, including the powerful *Hampshire, Minotaur, Melbourne* and *Ibuki,* hotly in pursuit of his *Emden,* almost insignificant by comparison.

Insignificant, and yet little *Emden* had captured or sunk twenty-four merchant ships, without harming a hair on the head of a single passenger or member of the crew, destroyed two enemy warships and raided installations of two major Middle Eastern ports. For days at a time shipping had been blocked in harbours, fearing to risk the open sea and the menace of a swift German raider which seemed to be lurking just off every roadstead.

By the laws of average, *Emden* should have exhausted her luck. And indeed, this morning, as von Müller scanned the horizon, this possibility grew into something stronger than speculation.

To the north, a wisp of smoke, which he had at first taken to be from his captive collier *Buresk*, plumed nearer with an alarming, growing insistence.

As he was to log:

'Soon we began to doubt . . . whether it could be the *Buresk*, as she was usually almost smokeless; but it was considered that the unusually dense smoke cloud might be attributed to her having had a fire in her bunkers the day before, which was probably causing her to use the partly burnt coal; moreover, she would certainly be running at top speed. From the crow's nest, too, it was at first incorrectly reported that the ship in sight had one funnel and two masts.

'At 9.15 the landing party showed no sign of returning, so I signalled to them: "*Arbeiten beschleunigen!*" (Speed up the work at hand.) Soon afterwards the masts of the oncoming vessel . . . were recognized as those of a warship on account of their height. Probably through an error she was not at first making direct for Port Refuge, but seemed to be trying to pass the group on the east side.

'What followed now happened extraordinarily quickly, as the enemy warship was coming on at high speed—twenty to twenty-five knots. I ordered steam up in all the boilers and repeated several times the recall for the landing party; then I gave the orders, "Up anchor! Clear ship for action! Get up steam immediately to put on all possible speed!"

'By this time it was seen that the enemy ship had four funnels, and we guessed it was the English cruiser, *Newcastle*; only in the afternoon did we discover that she was the Australian cruiser *Sydney*, a ship of very similar type.'*

On Direction Island, First Officer von Muecke, his landing party and Superintendent Darcy Farrant, of the cable station, heard *Emden*'s siren. It wailed with a frantic urgency. The cables had been dredged up and cut, the transmitting sets smashed into broken glass and bent metal, even the message paper strewn on to the floor like the litter of confetti and ticker tape after a parade.

The German sailors began to push their launch and skiff into the water, then paused. The smoke belched black from their cruiser's funnels, as the anchor chain clanked up out of the clean, coral-sand bottom. Muzzle covers were being snatched from the guns, ready boxes were thrown open, ammunition was passed to the waiting breeches.

'Schnell . . . !' von Muecke called to his coxswain. But it was too late.

With two short blasts of her siren the *Emden* leaped forward, suddenly parting the calm, blue water into two foaming bow waves.

---

* *Official History of Australia in the War of 1914–1918*, by Arthur W. Jont, Angus and Robertson, Ltd., Sydney.

Von Muecke pushed his hat slightly back from his sweating forehead and looked at Farrant. Farrant smiled quietly at him.

On board the cruiser, von Müller had reckoned it this way:

'About 9.30 a.m. the landing party began to re-embark, but, with the enemy quickly approaching, it was seen to be impossible to get them aboard before the fight began. As soon, therefore, as the anchor was weighed, I ordered full steam ahead and set the ship on a north-north-west course so as to improve still further our favourable position with regard to the wind until the actual beginning of the fight. My object was to attempt to inflict on the enemy such damage by gun-fire that her speed would be seriously lessened, and I might be able to bring on a torpedo action with some chance of success.'

Von Muecke embarked nonetheless. And Farrant recorded:

'Lieutenant von Muecke shook hands with me on leaving, and apologized for having to blow up our small engineer's store, owing to there being a roll of electric light cable there, and hoped the flames would not spread. All the men were looked over for loot, and a few minutes later put out to rejoin their ship.

'After the departure of the boats, I requested the staff to have breakfast and then help in clearing up and finding out exactly how we stood . . . a report was brought in that a large ship was approaching from the eastwards, and at the same time it was noticed that the *Emden* was standing out to sea.

'Getting on to the barrier, a cruiser was seen coming

up at a great rate, stoking heavily and enveloped in a cloud of black smoke.'

The *Sydney* was of approximately 6,000 tons, nearly twice the size of *Emden*. Her main battery of six-inch guns compared to the German's 4.1-inchers as a shotgun would to a boy's air rifle. Her top speed was twenty-six knots, at least one knot faster than *Emden*, and in battle one knot can spell defeat or victory.

Here was the terrible moment in a naval commander's existence—decisively outclassed, he could give battle, surrender or possibly scuttle his ship. There was no possibility of flight.

Von Müller was alone, with his ship, his men, and his God. He held no hope of survival, and he prayed softly.

Another odd circumstance: he did not even have to be in this predicament. He could be steaming off the coast of South America in the relative security of Admiral von Spee's powerful squadron, already the victor over the hapless British Admiral Cradock. But in August, von Müller, for his own reasons, had chosen to leave von Spee's impressive assemblage.

Now the *Sydney* altered to a converging course. The *Emden*'s gun crews were silent, holding ammunition in hands. They were ready.

The enemy was looming larger. Her four funnels were plainly discernible, the great length of her main-deck . . . distance now about 13,000 yards . . . bearing about four points on *Emden*'s starboard bow . . . moving in rapidly.

Gunners looked through the 'scopes . . . 12,000 yards, 11,500 . . . 11,000 . . . range closing fast . . . 10,500 . . . 10,000.

The gunners waited. Other than the straining speed of the engines, there was a close stillness like that which grips the China Seas before a typhoon strikes.

At 9,800 yards the order came—'Fire!'

With a doomsday shattering crash, a rush of heat, a gust of wind, the *Emden*'s first salvo thundered across the intervening space of calm Indian Ocean.

THE saga began on a pleasant afternoon in Tsingtao, June 28th, 1914. There, Karl von Müller walked the bright streets of the Kaiser's model North China coast colony, and had much to be thankful for, especially his command of two years, the cruiser *Emden*.

In a way, the story went even further back, to the emotional cosmos which sent a young boy from his home in Blankenburg, nestled in the christmas tree fairyland of the Harz, to become a naval cadet, and to wed himself to the sea and its fortunes.

A happy but pensive child, Karl inherited certain characteristics from both parents; his militia-officer father, a heavy, black-bearded man with stern eyes and sterner principles, and a warm, effervescent mother who might have played roles of princess on the stage had not she elected the more customary one of *Hausfrau*.

He was and he was not, in one paradoxical amalgam of personality, truly German. He was blond, erect, logical—but he loved Spanish music, and even to dance with señoritas when he was to call at Caribbean and South American ports as a cadet. He had a restrained sense of humour and could even laugh at himself.

But he was also shy, and seemingly possessed with a latent, semi-Wagnerian sadness, which could mask itself under a colder peremptoriness. Though he always

B   [17]

had friends, there was a loneliness in von Müller's heart— his sister, Elfreda, who was very close to him, attested to that.

He soon became a world-traveller. In 1891, he visited Niagara Falls. He had left his sailing ship *Gneisenau* in Newport and borrowed five dollars for train fare from his admiral. This quiet, young officer-in-training had early proven himself not only to be endowed with above-average curiosity, but boldness in the same proportion.

He had an unusually high degree of interest and understanding both in naval strategy and warship design. He also had no fear of expressing his ideas. Once he even discoursed on the ageless imponderables of fighting ships, 'weight-speed-armament', with the formidable von Tirpitz himself. He finally made the great admiral admit: '*Ach*, all ships are a compromise, at best. . . .'

He saw duty on many ships, including the tiny cruiser *Schwalbe* and the massive old battlewagon, *Kaiser Wilhelm II*, on which he was gunnery officer. He became acquainted with brother naval officers of almost all nations. In London he was entertained by royalty, and in Berlin, British naval attachés looked forward to his company. Count Zeppelin's son was a close friend. Always, his friends bore witness, he had a will to serve, to 'play the game', and above all, to be a gentleman and a human being. In sailing the seas for his Kaiser it was not so much a matter of blind allegiance but simple instinct.

In its curious way, fate (plus the navy) had brought von Müller to Tsingtao that June. There had been world tension for the past few weeks, but no one really seemed to want war. A long, prosperous peace had followed Bismarck's defeat of France and the German Empire was shaping up nicely, stretching into the Pacific Ocean and its firmament of islands.

It felt like any day on the China coast—bright, warm, sights almost out of a travel folder. Germany had built splendid schools, gymnasiums, government buildings and apartment houses, improved the harbour, erected power stations, a railway and forts on the surrounding hills. Even so, there were 40,000 Chinese to 2,500 Europeans and the sing-song personality of the Orient was very evident.

Von Müller walked along broad, paved Kuangsu Road, past its dignified, plaster residences, and the neatly trimmed rows of acacia and almond trees. They smelled rich and sweet, along with many other varieties of shrubs and flowers farther back in the hills. The Chinese were busy in their rocky little gardens, surrounded by lean, clucking chickens.

From the 1,000-foot elevation of Iltis Fortress, the strongest in Tsingtao's chain of harbour batteries, there was a beautiful perspective of the city, its crescent bathing beach, and the vessels warped to the docks or riding at anchor. They were all dominated by the old battleship *Kaiserin Elisabeth*.

Until evening, war seemed quite a distant possibility. Von Müller was eating dinner in the Marineverein when he heard the news: Archduke Francis Ferdinand, heir to the Austro-Hungarian throne, and his wife had been assassinated in tiny little Bosnia.

It swept the colony like a fire. By midnight many Tsingtao colonials were at the Prince Heinrich Hotel, filled with beer and singing patriotic songs like *Deutschland über Alles*! One exception was Karl von Müller, who, back on his ship, somehow knew that the sun which had risen on this June 28th, 1914, would ever afterwards rise on a different world.

July fled like a dream. No one any more doubted the world was readying for Armageddon, and in Tsingtao defence measures were accelerated. Lines of army trucks, laden with supplies, rumbled through the streets all day long and wound up the hillsides to the forts, leaving dusty wakes.

'They are impregnable,' many an army officer boasted. 'Tsingtao cannot be taken from the sea. No one would attempt it from the land.'

Von Müller, following emergency plans, had his officers systematically readying *Emden* for—anything. Furniture, woodwork, carpets, curtains, anything that would easily ignite was removed and stored in one of the warehouses along Kwangtung Road. Gunnery Officer Gaede fussed over the cruiser's armament night and day like a mother hen, polishing, disassembling, reassembling, greasing, modifying the precious equipment. Torpedo Officer Witthoeft was equally meticulous in his department, as was Navigating Officer Gropius in his, Dr. Luther, the surgeon, in his own. The rolls of medical dressings the latter brought aboard were, at least, sobering.

There was an exceptionally youthful—most in their early twenties—and distinguished group of officers on the *Emden*, including Francis Joseph von Hohenzollern, a distant nephew of the Kaiser.

Several times during the month the cruiser cast off

moorings and sped into the Yellow Sea for target prac-
tice. By evening, she would be boiling back in.

Life in the city assumed a heady exhilaration. People
waltzed half the night in the Prince Heinrich ballroom,
or clicked beer steins in the Marineverein or Volks-
verein. There was a run of withdrawals from the
Asiatic-German Bank.

Morals dropped somewhat below the level of a colony
even of Singapore's repute. Out on Kuangsu Road,
the incense burned and the temple bells tinkled beside
the bamboo curtains of many rooms where ecstasy could
be won for but a few marks. In amateur ranks, a few
wives found pleasant solution to temporary loneliness
while their naval or army officer husbands were
away.

On July 30th, a telegram arrived from Berlin warning
naval commanders of the increasingly serious international equilibrium. It was fast tilting. Von Müller
became grave. He conferred with his officers and soon
had a chain of coolies loading extra coal and ammunition on to his ship.

Their singing lent its own oriental charm to the scene
as they passed their burdens on board in an endless,
rhythmical human chain.

On the other side of the world, people, too, were
apprised of the precarious situation. Headlines in the
New York Times ran like this:

GERMAN SQUADRON STOPPING MERCHANT
    VESSELS IN DANISH WATERS
TOURISTS IN PARIS ARE IN WAR PANIC
BIG GERMAN LINES STOP ALL SHIPPING

LONDON EXCHANGE CLOSES ITS DOORS
DUTCH ARMY CALLED OUT
BELGIUM MOBILIZES
SWISS CALL TO ARMS
THINKS KAISER IS BLUFFING

In Pittsburgh, the German Davis Cup tennis team was soundly trounced by the Australian players.

But there was no time, now, for tennis matches in Tsingtao. At dawn, on July 31st, the *Kaiserin Elisabeth* raised her anchor and waddled ponderously out of the harbour.

At 7 p.m. the *Emden* followed, accompanied by the cargo ship *Elsbeth*. The latter broke off at midnight and steered south for a rendezvous with the *Kaiserin Elisabeth*. A main concern was not to be bottled up in Tsingtao if war should be declared and an enemy squadron steam in for a surprise bombardment.

The great Vladivostok base to the north, around the spur of Korea, posed its own threat. The heavy French cruisers *Montcalm* and *Dupleix* had recently been reported there. On the other hand, First Lord of the Admiralty Winston Churchill had unwittingly relieved German fears by ordering his East Asiatic Squadron to assemble at Hong Kong, far to the south.

On the morning of Sunday, August 2nd, the blow fell. *Emden* was well out in the Yellow Sea. Von Müller, after church services, mustered officers and crew on the poop-deck, then read quickly from a slip of paper:

'The following wireless message has just been received from Tsingtao, "On August 1st, His Majesty the Emperor

ordered the mobilization of the entire land and naval
forces of the Empire. Russian troops have crossed the
border into Germany. As a consequence, the Empire
is at war with Russia and with France! . . . The victory
will be no easy one".'

Three cheers were sounded for 'His Majesty the
Emperor', and the men dismissed. Von Müller confided
to his officers his initial plans.

The mission was to raid enemy commerce—that and
that alone. And, as an early sample of von Müller's
daring, he would push north toward the very enemy
lair which posed such a threat: Vladivostok.

If nothing else, *Emden* should perhaps encounter the
Russian mail steamer plying between Vladivostok and
Nagasaki and other shipping from Chinese ports. A
south-east course was set for the Straits of Tsushima,
between Korea and Japan. Condition three was in effect
—one-third of the crews constantly at their guns.

By evening the sea was a mirror. Blacked-out, the
Emden steamed into the Straits with the speed of some
bird which could almost, but not quite, fly off the surface.
There was no moon and the night was dark, except for a
shimmering, phosphorescent-green wake. These waters
were hazardous for navigation, studded with pin-point
islands, rocks and rocky spurs. Along the Korean coast,
just north, a vast island archipelago raised out of the
sea.

At midnight, tiny Pinnacle Island was winking ahead,
off the port bow . . . flashing every ten seconds. *Emden*
was right on track, and ready to alter course for Vladivostok to the north.

At 2 a.m. it was noted in the log that the wind was

freshening from the south. It smelled, with that indefinable prescience, like brewing typhoon weather. The *Emden* was taking a rhythmic quartering roll. She had a normal highspeed roll, as does any slender, fast vessel. Yet any salt could perceive what part of the roll was caused by the sea, and what by the 13,400 horsepower reciprocating engines that Blohm and Voss built.

At 4 a.m. all hands were awakened by the jangling of alarm bells. Thoughts centred on the *Montcalm* and the *Dupleix*, or the newest Russian battle cruiser *Sevastopol*, 23,300 tons, 12-inch guns, a deadly Goliath of the seas.

Smoke had been sighted dead ahead. As the *Emden* had drawn closer, the shape materialized into a medium-sized, darkened ship, which might have been a man-of-war.

She turned and ran immediately, streaming black smoke which lay on the water. Her speed could not have been more than five knots slower than *Emden*'s. In another hour it was light enough to reveal her as a modern cargo ship, two stacks, trim lines. The pennants were unfurled on *Emden*'s signal halyards. They ordered in international code:

'Stop at once!'

Her only answer was to alter course to the east, as though she might outrace them into some Japanese port.

'Load a blank!'

. . . third loader to second loader to first loader on the forward 4.1-inch 40 calibre, into the breech, lock the breech . . . sight setter, fire!

Blam! An empty, hollow sound, with no projectile.

The acrid smoke drifted back and stung eyes, then was washed away by a dash of spray from over the bow.

She did not stop, or slow down. And she was flashing out an S.O.S.

With all his patience, von Müller was now furious.

'Forward battery, open fire! First rounds high . . . !'

. . . from magazine to third loader to second loader to first loader, into the open breeches of two batteries . . . clicking of breech locks.

'Pointers, on target!'

'Sight setters, ready!'

'*Feuer*!'

Holding ears against the jolting crash of the salvo. The shells screamed over the vessel's masts, landed in the water just ahead, shooting neat geysers.

The ship broke out Russian colours on her topmasts . . . and hove to.

Senior Lieutenant Lauterbach was ordered into the cutter with twelve men. They carried pistols with the exception of one gunner who held a Maxim automatic gun in his lap. He contemplated it fondly as though it were a pet.

The sea was building up, dirty green and rougher all the time. The sailors had to manœuvre carefully to the merchantman over the crests and down into the troughs of the waves so as not to be swamped.

Alongside, the cutter was slapped against the towering sides of the steamer. Her crew, staring moon-faced over the railings, offered but passive assistance with mooring lines and fenders. Mindful of her reluctance to obey the first orders, the boarding party was prepared

[25]

for any treachery, even under the *Emden*'s covering guns.

Finally the raider's party climbed up the rope ladder, one by one, and sent the cutter back to the cruiser with only the coxswain aboard. The prize turned out to be the *Rjesan*, the Shanghai-Vladivostok mail-passenger steamer. She had recently been built in a north German shipyard and was registered as a Russian naval aux-iliary, accounting for her speed.

Her captain, indignant, protested 'violation' of inter-national law. Lauterbach, endeavouring to mollify him, assured him the *Rjesan* would not be sunk, but would be convoyed to Tsingtao for the Kaiser's service.

'Suppose I refuse?' the master asked.

Lauterbach laughed. He blinked back and forth with the *Emden* and finally, with instructions clear, started up, full-speed ahead, to trail the cruiser.

By afternoon a heavy sea was rolling up from the south and *Rjesan* was labouring. But there was nothing to do except push towards the China coast, away from enemy waters.

The green spray swept over the forepeak, past the kingposts and slapped against the glass ports of the navi-gation bridge. The air was warm, moist and full of menace.

About dusk, as the *Emden* rounded the southern tip of Korea, seven smoke clouds were spotted astern. This could have been the French fleet with the *Montcalm* and *Dupleix*. Now, nervous blinker lights began across the stormy waters in the gathering gloom. Dit-dit-dah . . . dah-dah-dah . . . International Morse spelled out the conversation.

The *Emden* was changing course, a wide southward circle; under the circumstances, and hemmed in by land masses—including Japan itself—there was no other choice. Von Müller was not ready yet to fight the whole French Asiatic fleet!

Once mantled by the night's blackness, the ship swung left to about 200 degrees compass, meeting the green combers head on. The two vessels commenced to pitch heavily. Plates clattered, silverware jingled and furniture slid in the saloons. The twenty-four passengers on the *Rjesan* were having an uncomfortable time. The captain protested again.

'I must,' he demanded, 'be taken to the nearest port!'

Of the passengers, more than half were Russian women —fat, ageing and, as it turned out, rather foolish. One gunner had at first spotted a light from an unscreened porthole. The particular cabin was occupied by two women, who giggled and stuck their tongues out at the Germans when they screened the ports.

In a few minutes, from the bridge wings, Lauterbach spotted light again shining from that port and from another on the opposite side. This time Lauterbach in person angrily removed the electric bulbs.

It wasn't the end. The fat women had taken bulbs from other cabins, for, sure enough, Lauterbach had hardly returned to the bridge when the lights started winking on again.

He sent a petty officer to the engine-room to pull fuses controlling the particular cabins. He then locked the women in their cabins after indicating in unmistakable sign language that he'd personally shoot the next one who might contrive a light. He tapped his Luger with his fingers as he spoke.

No more lights showed that night.

By morning, *Emden* had lost her pursuers, and outrun the worst of the storm—just a low, wet sky remaining, and a moderating swell from the west. The *Emden* was still ahead, about 2,000 yards, as she was the previous evening. She altered course towards Tsingtao once more.

After breakfast there came a great chattering from the wireless shack of the *Rjesan*, where one of the Germans was on guard to make sure no message was transmitted. The operator removed his headphones and hurried over to the captain, whispered something in his ear. The captain's fat face was wreathed in a sudden big, almost foolish smile.

'Great Britain,' he exulted, 'has just declared war on you.' He looked at Lauterbach as though he were a schoolboy who had been reprimanded.

In the afternoon another message was intercepted. The same radio operator had copied a press report from the British Reuters syndicate:

'. . . the *Emden* has been sunk by a powerful Asiatic squadron of His Majesty's Navy.'

The wireless man pointed to the slip of paper, then to the silhouette of the *Emden* steaming ahead, grinned a toothless grin and returned to his enforcedly silent job as monitor.

Early next morning *Emden* transited German mine-fields and brought her prize triumphantly into Tsingtao. Even as she warped to the railway dock, an officer came aboard and advised that the *Rjesan* would be armed as an auxiliary. They would start removing the guns at once from an older, slower, auxiliary, the *Kormoran*.

Germany's Asiatic base had redoubled its activity. Many more ships had fled into its sanctuary and lighters, sampans, all manner of harbour craft were rapidly unloading them. The streets and sidewalks were an ant-procession day and night of coolies, carrying supplies to stores, warehouses and on up the hillsides to the glowering forts with their gun snouts poking seaward. The air rang with a familiar Eastern discord of many natives working in unison, and little dust swirls were kicked up from the legion of bare, flat feet.

Uniforms had sprouted where no uniforms had been before—the reservists. The head waiter at the Prince Heinrich had proven to be an Unterleutnant in the military police and was already officially directing traffic along the inner quays. One could no longer walk a hundred yards without being challenged for an identity card.

A little teller at the Asiatic-German Bank was resplendent in his Oberleutnant zur See uniform, waiting to be assigned a ship. Even the women had kept pace by donning Red Cross uniforms, and chattered everywhere like slightly drunken magpies, overwhelmed by their importance.

Emden received sailing orders only three days after her return. She had taken on so many supplies that she appeared more like an overloaded tramp than a sleek man-of-war. There were shell cases tucked even under bunks, while additional torpedoes were lashed, like mute, greasy sharks, at the side of the decks against the bulkheads.

The date was August 8th, and *Emden* was ordered to

meet Admiral von Spee off Pagan Island, in the Marianas, north of Guam and 1,600 miles south-east of Tsingtao. There she would rendezvous with his heavy armoured cruiser squadron, led by the mighty *Scharnhorst* and *Gneisenau* (successor to von Müller's old training ship). Smaller cruisers like the *Nürnberg*, destroyers and auxiliaries would complete his South Pacific striking force. It was a formidable challenge to the shipping of Germany's enemies.

Emden cast off in the morning, accompanied by the armed auxiliary, *Eitel Friedrich*, a North German Lloyd liner, and the coaler *Markomannia*, of the Hamburg-America Line, and several lesser auxiliaries.

The ship's band tooted solemnly, 'The Watch on the Rhine' as the cruiser drew out from dock and slipped down the harbour. Cheers rang from the shore, men waved hats and women dabbed handkerchiefs to their eyes. There was unusual finality to this sailing.

The rows of neat houses dropped astern, the fresh green trees, the pink mist of morning still faintly cottoning the brown of the hills. The cruiser passed the modern government buildings, the well-kept barracks, more piers, until finally she was entering the Yellow Sea. Only the pounding surf on Tsingtao's outer rocks and the shrinking profile of a church steeple far aft whispered that *Emden* had ever been more than a sea waif which knew no land.

Not many hours out, the wireless man intercepted a babble of messages. They were decoded sufficiently to indicate that most of the British Asiatic Fleet was just over the horizon steaming for Hong Kong.

Emden kept on course, with doubled watches at the

guns, and did not rest easily until the messages grew perceptibly fainter. His Majesty's Navy had missed a chance.

That same evening, a Japanese mail steamer wallowed close by. Germany was not at war with Japan. And, as von Müller had anticipated, she had barely disappeared over the horizon when her wireless began to crackle:

'German cruiser *Emden*, accompanied by auxiliaries, on course 135 degrees, approximately 190 miles from Tsingtao . . . !'

Emden altered course and stepped up convoy speed another knot. She was below her maximum since the older ships could not approach twenty-five knots. By morning she was reaching out of the East China Sea and into the vaster reaches of the Pacific.

The water was blue, flat and seemingly endless. It was almost empty of ships. Von Müller had been expecting the Canadian Pacific liner, *Empress of Japan*— a fat prize, but the Japanese mail steamer had undoubtedly warned her off.

Late on August 12th, the rendezvous was accomplished with the impressive ships of Admiral Spee's squadron. There was much blinking back and forth between the assemblage off Pagan Island. Finally von Müller entered his cutter and steamed to the Admiral's flagship.

Within an hour he was back, satisfaction on his face. He had received permission to detach the *Emden* and raid enemy shipping alone.

'Full speed' once more was signalled, and as *Emden* turned to the south-west, away from the squadron, the yellow, nervous light winked from the *Scharnhorst*'s signal lamp:

[31]

'Proceed, *Emden*!   God speed and *auf Wiedersehen*!'

Captain von Müller had chosen the loneliest course of command—that of a raider, operating entirely by herself, which would inevitably become the very kind of prey herself that she was seeking.   Yet his reasons for such a choice he never confided to his fellow officers.

Emden

The Cocos Islands

NEARLY a week was spent cruising leisurely southward and westward down the string of Marianas Islands. The squat *Markomannia* steamed faithfully in *Emden*'s wake.

Von Müller did not expect activity here; rather, he was taking time to think, and plan carefully. He was demonstrating once again that he was, curiously enough, both deliberate and daring.

Rumours cropped up throughout the ship, from the officers' wardroom to the crew's fo'c'sles. The *Emden* would raid here, would raid there—even the coastal shipping lanes of the United States itself. Von Müller merely smiled when he heard them.

It was a peaceful period. There was wine and beer on board, even a few magnums of champagne, consumed, off-watch, in moderation. Soap and hot water abounded, and the crew kept cool, neat and clean in light, tropical clothes. Von Müller had frequently said the happiness and health of his crew came first, adding that he would even consider stealing, if necessary, to see that his men were fed properly.

There was music and singing, and time to write letters home, even though no one knew how long they would be in transit, once posted. Wireless operators copied down the news every night and it was ready in the morning, typed on the bulletin boards.

News, indeed, was spectacular. German troops were already in Brussels. The opposing armies, even their mighty forts like Liége, had melted before the Kaiser's onslaught.

Days were hot, sometimes blistering as the lone cruiser drove ever southward to meet the Equator. At night, von Müller throttled back, and tried to steam on a course which afforded a breeze, even though slight.

The sea was immensely blue and calm off the Marianas. A fish could jump out of water 3,000 feet abeam and the ripples would continue to spread as in a pond. Sometimes the *Emden* would weave through dozens of tiny tropical thunderstorms, pin-pointed as far as the eye could see like dark cotton balls. Between them the sun shone resplendently.

This was the latitude of albatrosses and frigate birds. They wheeled, usually one at a time, high above the masts, kept easily aloft by wings that spread as wide as twelve feet. There was something ominous about them—these magnificent silent vultures of the open sea.

All hands ate well—sausages, fresh eggs, ham, good dark bread baked daily—and gained weight.

During this time, von Müller had been trying to contact the German cable and wireless station on the Island of Yap, westernmost of the Carolines. Soon he became concerned, and decided to put in at this tiny bit of volcanic earth and investigate.

On August 18th the *Emden* was passing Entrance Rock, on the east side of the ten-mile wide, low-lying island. She crept into Tomil Bay as far as the navigator dared, not trusting the charts of this area of underwater coral.

One jagged reef could rip a keel as effectively as a torpedo.

The *Emden* anchored in mid-channel. The light, coffee-coloured natives in their outrigger canoes soon swarmed around, jabbering in rising and falling excitement. It was impossible to understand what these Micronesians, naked save for loin cloths, were trying to convey. A landing party went ashore in a cutter, to talk with Yap's small German colony.

The cutter chugged in, half the outrigger fleet following. The youngest, strongest swimmers dived from their light, frail craft, and stroked ahead. They were waiting at the little wharf, with its bamboo roof, lines in hand.

The German party walked along a path of crushed shells, lined with palms, up to a settlement. The houses were built on stilts, as protection against typhoon tides, of fibres and native wood, with peaked, thatched roofs that seemed higher than necessary. One structure, with a distinct European flavour to its architecture, carried over the porch steps a sign, 'Jaluit Trading Co.'

A middle-aged, obese man puffed out to meet the visitors. He wore a sun helmet, almost standard dress in the islands, and his shirt was open, exposing a thick growth of hair, matted to his chest with sweat.

'I'm Schmidt,' he said, without preliminaries. 'I'm temporarily in charge of the company. Come, this way. I will show you.'

He hurried past the clearing and through the jungle, up a slight rise of ground. He did not stop until he had reached a much smaller clearing, on what might be described as a summit—if an island as close to the water as Yap could possess summits, or valleys.

In the middle were charred, twisted ruins of wood timbers, steel work, and wire.

'This was the cable and wireless station,' Schmidt announced.

A German youth was groping in the midst of the rubble, pushing the wreckage away, lifting up a blackened, bent bit of equipment to examine it.

'Only twelve days ago, three British cruisers came in here,' the trader continued. 'They were the *Hampshire*, *Yarmouth* and *Minotaur*. They bombarded this wireless station, then sailed away.'

Finally the *Emden* party returned to the dock. The signalman with his portable blinker light flashed back and forth with the *Emden*, riding majestically at anchor and dominating the whole island. The party would stay ashore for the night, on the highest point of ground, while the engineers made minor repairs to boiler tubing.

The afternoon passed. The German sailors wandered this pungent, luxuriant island and learned about the peace-loving, gentle Micronesians who called Yap home.

The foreign colony had dwindled to a handful of copra traders, Spanish as well as German, like Herr Schmidt. Others had started leaving six months ago, fearing the advent of war. As for the native Micronesians, there were not over five thousand now on Yap.

Their society was idyllic. When not fishing, they sat around—men, women and children—smoking cigarettes, chewing betel nuts and listening to old gramophone records. The 'canned' music machine itself they called the 'tom-tom'.

In the evening they danced the *tsuru*—one version

seated, which told a story of canoe heroes by gesticulations of hands and arms and changes of facial expressions. The standing version of the *tsuru*, for some reason, was considered unfit for the ladies, who discreetly padded off splay-footed to their houses when the men performed it. It was assumed that most of the women peeked.

Many of the men lived in long, barracks-like huts, *failus*. They were either bachelors or males who felt their families had no immediate need of them, and the whole lot shared one, or at the most two, mistresses. Jealousy was unknown in Yap.

Most Micronesians were shy at first, but tried to become friends, once they knew the visitors' mission was not to interfere with their life or customs. No money was of interest, other than pretty trinkets. The *fei* was the medium of exchange—large stone wheels, with a hole in the centre. The master with the most and biggest *feis* in front of his hut was also the wealthiest.

The women held little appeal for westerners. They were dressed not much more plenteously than the men, except for necklaces of hibiscus fibre twined loosely and shirts of dried leaves and strips of bast that appeared tremendously inflammable. They tended to plumpness.

Darkness came quickly as the *Emden* sailors stood watch. From the rich, colourful glow of evening—it was night. The jungle noises commenced, the cries of nocturnal birds, the chatter of apes, the gathering pound of the sea on the outer coral reefs as the winds shifted, and, for a few hours, the cries and thump-thumping rhythm as the people of Yap danced the *tsuru*.

Overhead the sky was bright with stars. The Southern

Cross was a resplendent beacon. Once in a while, fiery-tailed meteorites streaked high across the heavens . . . and the naval war, moving on that August, swept across the world's seas, even to the once peaceful Caribbean. The *Dresden*, sister ship of the *Emden*, boldly captured, though later released, the British steamer *Hostilius* off Cienfuegos, Cuba. Two days later, another Britisher, *Hyades*, fell victim to her.

In history's first battle between armed luxury liners, the Cunarder *Carmania* sank the German *Cap Trafalgar* off Trinidad. The latter was a flaming coffin when she took her last plunge, still refusing to surrender. The loss of life was appalling.

Not far away, 200 miles south of Bermuda, the *Karlsruhe* decided to fight another day as she churned in escape from the *Suffolk*.

In European waters, the *Goeben* and *Breslau* exchanged sporadic fire with the *Gloucester*, then broke off a desultory battle. And the *Königsberg* was playing a cat-and-mouse game with merchant and war ships alike off the African coast.

The auxiliary liner, *Kaiser Wilhelm der Grosse*, was sunk by the English cruiser *Highflyer* near the Rio de Oro, off north-west Africa.

CHAPTER 4

D AWN was streaking the eastern rim of ocean when the *Emden* signalled her crew to return; and they, having finished with their long night vigil, hurried back to the cutter.

Repairs had been made and von Müller was anxious to push on to another German colony, Angaur, less than a day's steaming to the south. There he planned to rendezvous with the *Prinzessin Alice*, a North German Lloyd mail steamer, which radioed she had Naval Reservists aboard.

A hot, calm run followed to Angaur, sighting nothing. The *Emden* dropped anchor in the harbour at dinner time, several hundred yards astern of the squat *Prinzessin Alice*. Immediately she put a launch over the side, and in a few minutes, ten enlisted men and two junior officers laden with seabags were climbing aboard the *Emden* to augment her crew.

The *Prinzessin Alice* carried an amazingly diverse cargo, including nearly a million English pounds sterling. Caught at sea when the war broke out, her captain saw no moral obligation to complete its delivery to Hong Kong.

She also had a supply of American newspapers. The latter, however, did not wholly entertain for, as one officer asserted, 'the contents were so imbecile that we could hardly believe them, consisting as they did of sensationalism and typically American stock exchange manœuvres.'

At nightfall, her captain came aboard the *Emden*. The tiny island was disappearing into the gloom, as beach fires began to pin-prick the darkness. The natives were cooking dinners of fish and bread fruit.

The *Prinzessin Alice*'s master told von Müller that a British freighter, loaded with 7,000 tons of phosphate, had just sailed from the island. There was not so much as a rifle to defend Angaur, let alone patrol boats.

Von Müller became increasingly apprehensive in these waters. His guest barely had time for a bottle of beer before he was hurrying back to his ship. In less than half an hour, the *Prinzessin Alice*'s anchor chain clanked up from the sandy bottom. Her hulking form, dark as the night itself, glided toward open sea. Von Müller did not believe she could keep up with *Emden* and, as senior naval officer, had ordered the merchant skipper to head north for neutral Cebu, in the Philippines.

Aboard the mail steamer, appropriately enough, was a letter from von Müller to Blankenburg:

Dearest Mother,

Will these lines reach you? Perhaps in six weeks, and that will be your birthday.

I cannot discuss our operations since this letter may fall into enemy hands. I wonder how the happenings in Germany on the east and west frontiers stand, and if the naval warfare in the North Sea, which apparently has begun so auspiciously, has spread farther.

We are many days without news of home. . . .

In the morning *Emden* rendezvoused with an antiquated German gunboat, the *Geier*. She was far too slow, a liability. Von Müller ordered her to proceed east to Honolulu and be interned rather than needlessly sacrifice his men in an encounter.

Shortly after the *Geier* lumbered over the horizon, leaving a smoke-smudge in her wake, a deep-laden Japanese freighter passed close by, steering on a northerly course. Colours were dipped. Von Müller ignored the pleasantry, assuming that Japan would soon be in the war. Only the legal technicality of time, restrained him from sinking her, since he was convinced she was laden with cargo for the British.

On August 23rd, Japan finally declared against Germany and attacked Tsingtao—blockading the harbour with units of her fleet, sending seaplanes aloft to reconnoitre. The hearts of the German sailors became heavy with the news; Tsingtao was their home, its people their countrymen.

If it should fall, *Emden* would be without a base.

The cruiser swept on, west and south, and south-west, snaking through the maze of South Pacific islands . . . paralleling the north-west coast of New Guinea, noting in amazement the hugh *lakatois*, ocean-going canoes, with their horn-like sails putting far out to sea from New Guinea's coasts, then transiting the Halmahera Straits . . . congested, perilous waters where the English fleet might appear at any moment.

The full moon was almost in phase and even blackout became of little avail at night time. The crew slept with considerably less assurance than had been their custom.

A few days later the ship cruised down the Banda Sea

and into Koepang Bay, Dutch Timor. The *Emden* had been consuming *Markomannia*'s coal gluttonously; the collier was riding high out of the water. Von Müller had to replenish her storage bins and the bunkers for *Emden*'s furnaces.

Timor presented a geographical contrast to the flat Pacific islands which had rimmed the cruiser's course. It was mountainous, somewhat reminiscent of Tsingtao. Some of the old volcanic upheavals reared a mile heavenward behind the Bay.

The anchor had scarcely clanked down to the pebbly harbour bottom when a launch approached. Immaculate in his whites, a Dutch officer stepped aboard. After saluting and identifying himself as from the battleship *Tromp*, he continued in excellent German:

'The Admiral's compliments . . . and he regrets that Holland, because of our strict neutrality, cannot allow a warship of any belligerent to remain.' He paused, to glance over the somewhat sea-weary *Emden*, 'I must ask you to depart at once.'

Gone were the sailors' visions of a night ashore, Bol's gin and cherry brandy . . . native girls.

Von Müller thanked him coolly. The Dutch officer left and the *Emden* steamed out of Koepang Bay and Timor, threading between the maze of coral reefs.

However, less than a day's run brought the cruiser to Portuguese territory where she coaled. It was a poor grade of fuel, and the quantity was limited, but it would satisfy the cruiser's fiery appetite for at least another week. It was better than fouling furnaces with wood, which could be chopped in an emergency.

The *Emden* was speedily on her way again, pushing

[42]

closer to the Indian Ocean, a 'British lake'. This sanctuary would be *Emden*'s hunting preserve. It was a thoroughfare for the Empire and for nations which supplied it, as busy in its own waterborne traffic as Unter den Linden, in Berlin, was in its type of traffic.

That started inventive-minded officers thinking. German cruisers had three funnels; standard equipment like two ears, two eyes, a nose and a mouth in a human. On the other hand, English cruisers, largely because of their increased length and more boilers, tended to four funnels.

The answer: make a dummy funnel!

While the *Emden* poked around Lombok Straits and later the Sunda Straits, off Batavia, between the Indian Ocean and the Java Sea, the officers worked feverishly on the project; building a funnel out of canvas and light lumber. When it was completed, the carpenter added hinges, the Bos'n paint, and it was secured in place, aft of No. 3 funnel. It was, in conception, the genius of von Muecke.

A few tugs on a rope and up it would come. The *Markomannia*, surveying the handiwork from all angles and distances, was finally satisfied of its authenticity.

'You look like the bloody *Yarmouth*—blokes!' the coaler's skipper flashed.

The next day, *Emden* was steaming in that lonely expanse between the tip of Sumatra and the Cocos Islands, far to the south. Wireless messages were intercepted from an English ship—it was searching for German raiders.

One shore station bluntly asked: '*Emden*, where are you?'

Von Müller moved endlessly between the radio shack and the navigation bridge. The wireless was his second brain, a source of naval intelligence. Few enemy vessels possessed superior radio equipment. Through its tremendous range and clarity a wide cross-section of transmissions were overheard. By piecing them together, von Müller kept informed of the enemy's counter-measures, and the approximate positions of his naval and merchant ships.

The *Hampshire* was soon identified, and became almost garrulous. But, she was three times *Emden*'s tonnage, and her main battery was nearly twice the latter's calibre.

Yet, von Müller was drawn toward this warship with a mortal fascination. He altered course in her direction.

This was September 1st, four weeks since the capture of *Rjesan*. The crew were strangely glad to sniff the possibility of action lurking somewhere on the horizon, even if the odds were overwhelmingly against them. Exhilarating little fears crept into their minds.

All respected the fighting qualities of His Majesty's Navy. The raw courage and the ability of the Navy of Drake and of Nelson was unchanged through the years—they would fight until the waters closed over forepeaks. They would battle against odds that other sea forces could decline, honourably.

The *Emden* sped on, 'homing' by wireless on the *Hampshire*, even though von Müller knew that her captain, H. W. Grant, was a wily foe.

By late afternoon, with the fourth funnel in place, *Emden* was nearing Sumatra. First the mast lookout saw it, then it was picked up from the bridge with binoculars

. . . a wisp of smoke on the horizon, fast mushrooming into a sizeable, black smudge. Von Müller signalled for one-third speed.

The wireless man completed his 'fix'. There was the mighty *Hampshire*. The men stared in her direction over their loaded guns.

They could not afford to meet her by day, perhaps not even at night. Von Müller paced his bridge, lost in thought. He was spoiling to go in after her, guns blazing. But he knew that her superior range would be straddling his command several thousand yards before the *Emden*'s shells would be dropping close to the *Hampshire*.

All evening the *Emden*'s sailors watched her lights. It seemed almost a trick that she should be so exposed. Conversation lulled into ominous silence. Gramophones were clicked off and card games halted. In the laundry even the Chinese cackle of conversation grew unaccustomedly silent.

The crew listened to the whoom-whoom of the steam pistons, throbbing, up-down, up-down, and felt the easy sway of the decks as the *Emden*, like a reined racehorse, moved in, poised, waiting.

Shortly before midnight, the *Hampshire* started talking with the Dutch island of Simalur, off the north-west coast of Sumatra, a few score miles over the horizon. She was putting in there, perhaps to fuel.

Towards morning, the British cruiser pulled away. Her lights winked out over the horizon. Tension relaxed.

But the *Emden* hovered thirty miles off Simalur all that day and the next night. As far as could be ascertained the *Hampshire* remained somewhere in the island's shelter. Finally, von Müller decided to steam in.

'We must anchor in the bay,' he announced, 'and transfer coal from the *Markomannia*.'

On the morning of September 3rd, the *Emden* raised the coast of Simalur. Every man was at his gun station, the guns loaded, dummy funnel in place, the much slower *Markomannia* on the horizon, ready to flee. The *Emden* came in fast, in case she had to wheel and go out again. Native outriggers, which began to dot the waters, rode up and down like corks in the surging wake. Their occupants hung on and gaped.

As the charts showed, Simalur was a poor anchorage, exposed to the sea; not a true harbour but a long, oval bay. In heavy weather, it would be no good. Von Müller reduced speed and scanned the bay . . . nothing to be seen of the *Hampshire*.

He blinked astern at the *Markomannia* to follow. Off the south-east shore, only several hundred yards from a cluster of native huts, he signalled 'Stop!' to the engine-room and let go the anchor. Gun watches were reduced.

The German sailors felt a renewed sense of security. They were sheltered and believed, cradle-like, that nothing could harm them. Soon, when ears became acute again from the deafening throb of engines, lap-lap of water coursing along steel sides and other familiar, penetrating ship noises, the men heard the sounds from the thick, lush jungle which stretched inland from the waters edge. It was a blending of many sounds: birds, animals, the natives at work, and the soft, continual sighing of an animate jungle.

The *Markomannia* was warped alongside within the hour and the tedious transferring of coal commenced. Now it would be piled in special wooden bins on deck, to increase steaming range should the *Markomannia* be lost. Merchant Captain W. Paass came aboard to call on von Müller.

Von Müller had his men busy with other projects, too —ones filled with foreboding. Stripped were any remaining woodwork or curtaining from larger cabins such as the officers' wardroom. This was to reduce the danger of fire in battle. In the wardroom itself—a grim addition. There were two spare five-pounders (.55 calibre) in one of the *Markomannia*'s storage lockers. One was mounted on the deck, with its snout protruding from a portside porthole of the wardroom, the other from a starboard. This would increase firepower, if not a sense of normalcy as the officers read and sipped cocoa.

All but a very few senior officers must give up their quarters. This would serve a dual purpose: extra storage room for the ammunition coming aboard from the *Markomannia*, and space for the prisoners from captured ships.

Officers swung hammocks in a corner of the mess hall, though most nights they would sleep on deck. Blacked-out and with the engines pulsing at full speed, the hall would be an inferno of sweltering heat.

The work continued all that day: the rattle of coal bags, the irritating miasma of acrid dust, the banging, ripping and moving as the *Emden* was rearranged below decks. Dark-skinned natives paddled alongside to barter coconuts, coral jewellery and evil-looking bottled liquids for soap, tobacco, other luxuries. Otherwise, *Emden* was left quite alone in her south-east anchorage of Simalur's curving bay.

In the late afternoon, while men stood watch with high-powered rifles as protection against sharks, the sailors took turns swimming in the warm, clear waters. They dived under and tapped their hands against the cruiser's plates. She had already picked up a heavy sheathing of barnacles. It would fetter the *Emden*, beyond a doubt.

Under shaded lamps, the coal passing continued all evening. By 11 p.m., with 450 tons aboard, the men had to quit from breathless exhaustion. Everybody, except for the look-outs and a skeleton gun watch, turned in.

Hours later a wild screeching brought men upright in their hammocks. Hearts pounded. Then someone began to chuckle. The screeching settled into a throaty, exultant purring—Victoria, the cat who'd shipped on the last sailing from Tsingtao, had captured a rat and was playing with it. The sailors wondered how many rodents were disembarking from the somewhat less immaculate *Markomannia*.

Victoria had been the subject of previous speculation. When would she have kittens? She was hauling down lower and lower, 'midships, and her time was approaching. Some had already placed small wagers on the date.

At 6 a.m. coal transferring continued.

At 7.45 the look-out called: 'Launch approaching!'

In fifteen minutes it was alongside; a government yacht flying the Dutch flag. The officer, bald, explosive and little, wasted no time in pleasantries.

The radio mast, after it had been destroyed by
von Muecke's landing party

The landing party attempting to return to the *Emden*

H.M.A.S. *Sydney*

'You must get out at once!' he ordered. 'A belligerent warship cannot coal in Dutch waters!'

'Even to transfer our own coal?' von Müller asked.

'Even that!' he snapped. Then he looked up at the stacks. 'You have four funnels, like an English cruiser, and a German crew, a German flag, astern . . . ?' He threw up his hands, then walked down the steeply-sloping gang-plank without awaiting an explanation.

Emden, with close to 1,000 tons aboard, got under way again.

In the next few days radio traffic increased heavily, almost to a jumble of noise and static. *Emden* was nearing the busy shipping lanes in the Indian Ocean, fabled as a rich life-line of Empire since East Indiamen days. The night of September 9th, *Emden* arrived off Point de Galle, at the south-west tip of Ceylon. It was rough, misty weather, all hands were forced to wear waterproof jackets. Hammocks had to be swung in the stifling mess halls. Men slept in their broiling fo'c'sles.

Here sandalwood perfumed the heavy, tropical air. The urge to set foot on land welled like a frustrating hunger in everyone.

Soon, Galle Light, flashing twice every fifteen seconds. *Emden* was about sixteen miles to sea. Galle Harbour, other than being enemy territory, presented no great attraction. It was a shallow, open anchorage. The Ceylon Government Railway ran along the coast, in plain sight from the sea in daylight.

One officer suggested the *Emden* shell the railroad in the morning, perhaps blow up a freight train. Von Müller shook his head.

D

'This is not the artillery,' he stated gravely. 'Our one reason for existence is to harass and destroy enemy shipping—and we must do so until our means for waging sea warfare is exhausted, until we ourselves are destroyed.'

He spoke grimly. Yet another officer persisted. He pointed to the chart, fifteen miles down the coast, east of Point de Galle, and a wireless in the hills beyond Dondra Head.

'That station must be important, judging from the amount of traffic it is sending into the air,' he declared. 'Should we knock it out?'

Von Müller shook his head.

'The reefs,' he asserted. 'We could not come in close enough for safety to range it. Also, it has given us helpful information about enemy shipping.'

That night, as the *Emden* rolled cork-like in the ground swell, a ship appeared, shining like a beacon through the mist.

'Stop at once!' von Müller called through the megaphone.

The other craft continued ahead, switching off lights and altering course.

'Stop!' von Müller repeated. 'Do not use your wireless! We are sending a boat!'

Still no answer.

'Fire!' von Müller ordered.

A blank shot echoed through the night, across choppy Indian waters. Gunners held a 'live' shell, with projectile, in readiness for the next round.

The siren wailed suddenly from the strange vessel. She reversed engines, and began blinking her signal light:

'This is the Greek steamer *Pontoporos*.'

Emden had stumbled on a neutral. The reward: a wireless description of the *Emden*'s exact position. British fleet units at Trincomallee, on the east coast of Ceylon, Colombo, on the west, could be alerted. Nonetheless, a boat was sent over for her captain, as the watch officer thumbed Lloyd's Register of Merchant Shipping.

There was such a freighter, 4,049 tons, operated by the National Steam Navigation Co., of Greece, Ltd. That indicated the English had an interest in her.

In spite of the rough sea, the captain came safely on board.

'My God, a German cruiser here!' he exclaimed. 'The newspapers reported you had been lost six weeks ago!'

He identified himself as Captain D. Polemis, his home port, Andros, Greece. He admitted reluctantly that 6,500 tons of coal had been taken aboard at Calcutta.

'For the British fleet, of course,' von Müller suggested.

It was Indian coal, among the 'dirtiest in the world', except perhaps South African. It would clog the grates with clinkers.

'You won't mind joining our company for a time?' von Müller invited Captain Polemis.

He did object. He repeated he was flying a neutral flag. Von Müller, just as firmly, reminded him that his cargo was far from neutral, and would aid the enemies of Emperor Wilhelm.

Pontoporos involuntarily joined the 'fleet', flying the German colours, with one of *Emden*'s officers in command, her wireless sealed. She had already contributed something as valuable as coal: recent Calcutta newspapers, filled with sailing notices. It revealed, at a glance, where roughly every ship bound from that port should now be.

The crew also learned in detail how the war was going. Brief reports from the wireless now were confirmed and elaborated on. The news was dramatic: General von Hindenburg had defeated the invading Russian forces at Tannenberg, and thrown them back in full retreat; on the western front, German armies under von Kluck had swept within twenty-five miles of Paris and were fighting furiously along the Marne; the beautiful French capital was in a state of siege.

The British announced that they had sunk three German cruisers and two destroyers off Heligoland. A Reuter report described the burning of the university town of Louvain, Belgium, and execution of civilians.

In Parliament there was a growing demand for an explanation of how the cruisers *Goeben* and *Breslau* had successfully escaped through the Straits of Messina to the Dardanelles. There the two were now a part of the Turkish fleet. It was rumoured that Rear Admiral Ernest Charles Trowbridge, commanding the British Squadron in the Mediterranean, would be called to London.

While the *Emden* steamed eastward again across the Bay of Bengal, another English warship was identified— the cruiser *Minotaur*. As the *Hampshire*, she would be more than a match. Her signals indicated she was close by.

Von Müller watched the northerly horizon as his little warship tossed in the stormy seas. Rain slanted coldly, blindly across the thick glass portholes.

'Nothing new, Mr. Gropius?' he asked his navigating officer from time to time. 'Nothing new . . . ?'

'Nothing new,' would come the reply.

CHAPTER 5

S HORTLY after daybreak, September 10th, on a
course between Ceylon and the Nicobar Islands,
Emden sighted the masts, funnels and smoke smudge
of a steamer dead ahead. The rain had ceased, leaving
sullen, low skies and a choppy sea.

She was challenged by blinker at 5,000 yards and was
quick to reply. She was the *Indus*. And, when asked
further questions, she also complied: bound from
Calcutta for Bombay, to pick up troops and horses for
France. As an afterthought, her signalman added:

'We took you for a British cruiser!'

The fourth funnel had proved more of a success than
its inventor, von Muecke, had any right to expect.

While the *Emden* steamed off to investigate another
approaching vessel, Lieutenant Klopper was sent to the
Indus with a boarding party. A warrant officer, an
expert in demolition, and three stokers accompanied
him.

The *Indus* was smaller than the *Pontoporos*, sister to
thousands of similar-sized truck horses of the Seven Seas,
picking up a bit of cargo here, delivering it there, never
coming permanently alight, save to refuel, reprovision
and, but rarely, to have her sides and superstructure
painted.

George Read, second officer of the *Indus*, was stiffly
correct. His crew sullenly chewed tobacco and looked

the other way as members of the German boarding party passed them.

'Signal books?' Klopper asked.

Read led him to the bridge and pointed, with subdued satisfaction, to the empty file cabinets. The *Indus'* helmsman, in turn, broke into a grin as he gestured toward the ocean.

Then, as Klopper read the freighter's manifest, his face lit up. She was carrying a choice cargo when measured by a lone raider's physical wants: soap by the ton, towels, linen, tinned and fresh meat, live hens and ducks, beer, wine, gin, whisky, nautical instruments, charts, pencils, oilskins. . . .

Klopper set his three stokers to loading samples from the cargo into the *Emden's* cutter. He was particularly interested in soap. A regular naval officer, like von Müller, the lieutenant knew the importance of aseptic cleanliness to a ship's personnel.

While his petty officer went about the task of smashing tubes in the wireless, Klopper hurried below to the engine room. He ordered topsides all but the chief engineer, who was needed as a guide through the narrow passages of the cramped world of grease, hot metal, steam and coal fumes. He also wanted to learn the location of the sea valves.

The chief engineer proved either to have more curiosity than Read, or to be less able to contain it.

'You must be a ghost,' he observed, glancing at the stencilled letters *EMDEN* on the small case of demolition materials Klopper was carrying. 'We heard you were sunk two weeks ago, in the Pacific.' Then he lapsed into a seafarer's penchant for reminiscing.

'. . . think I saw you chaps last in Hong Kong, in the spring of 1913. We were bringing in a load of pump machinery. Right?'

But Klopper was already too busy to reply. With a huge wrench, he had removed from its hooks on the bulkhead, he was unscrewing the metal cap from the main bilge pipe. When finally it came loose, a geyser of water shot upward with a roar. The two men ducked.

Next, Klopper fastened open the water-tight doors leading to the engine room and placed two small dynamite charges against the port and starboard sides of the hull. He lit slow fuses and made sure the sparks were sizzling from them before he returned to the ladder.

'Hurry on ahead!' he told the chief engineer. Klopper felt honour-bound to be the last to leave the engine-room should there be a premature explosion. The water splashed and sloshed as it crept up to the open, glowing furnace doors.

'I haven't opened the boiler valves,' the chief engineer observed, looking over his shoulder, worried. 'The boilers might go when the cold water hits 'em, you know.'

'I am sorry,' Klopper said, 'but that's what I hope.'

The last members of the crew were leaving their fo'c'sles as Klopper gained the deck. Each man was allowed one duffel, each officer one suitcase. There had been little time to pack; now, with the fuses smouldering, there was less time to abandon.

One A.B. had somehow found the time to dress in his blue 'liberty' suit, felt hat and necktie. Another seaman, a Lascar, carried a parrot on his shoulder. The Chinese cook tucked a cat under each arm.

A young cadet was carrying, of all things, a faded brown framed picture under his arm. It was of a cottage, surrounded by high hedges, possibly his home.

Now the *Emden*'s cutter resembled a general store. It had made one trip to the cruiser and now was back for its second, and last. Assorted cardboard cartons of soap, linen and other essential items once consigned to the English, were topped by several crates of cackling hens and quacking ducks.

Two of the *Indus*' own boats were about to put out for the *Markomannia*, which would perform the temporary function of prison ship.

Meanwhile, the *Emden* had challenged another vessel, the *Lovat*, which stumbled across the scuttling of the *Indus*. The *Lovat* was bound for Bombay to embark troops. Her captain, a man of sixty, knew the *Emden*'s boarding officer, an ex-merchant mariner himself. The two men sat down for a brief drink of Scotch before abandoning the freighter.

'War is war,' the British master observed philosophically.

From the *Emden* the sailors watched the *Indus* sink. After the dynamite charges had detonated, the freighter began to lunge from side to side, like a pendulum, settling lower all the time. By the time the water was up to her decks, the *Lovat* nearby, also doomed, began to rock.

The *Indus* dipped by the bow as she assumed a list to starboard. She shivered as her stern, exposing a motionless propeller, pointed skyward. Her masts momentarily lay almost flat above the crests of the waves—the sea remained rough—and then only her funnel poking above the water.

There she paused long enough to blow out a puff of steam and smoke—and was gone, downward, like an arrow. She would not stop until she was resting on the sandy bottom of the Bay of Bengal. Ventilators, hatches, side windows, life preservers and crates plumed upward in a fountain-like spray from the air pressure released within the sinking ship. These were followed, in seconds, by large pieces of wreckage, spars and oars which were projected upward with great force . . . finally, a seething mound of water strewn with debris to mark the spot.

The *Indus* had gone.

From the safety of the *Markomannia*, her crew found it a sad spectacle. No sailor likes to watch the death of a ship, especially his own.

The *Lovat* was close behind her. The bow of this larger transport-to-be had disappeared as the waters closed forever above the *Indus*. Yet, von Müller was not quite satisfied with the way the *Lovat* was plunging and he ordered several shells rocketed into her side.

The *Lovat*'s stern was barely afloat, when the *Trabboch*, out of Liverpool, for Calcutta, appeared. Slightly larger than the *Indus*, she soon met the same fate. In ballast, she was a less valuable prize.

Emden intercepted a radio signal and took off twenty miles to the north-west—and captured the biggest prize yet, the *Diplomat*. The 7,600-ton Harrison Liner was carrying half again her weight in tea—for England.

Her captain, H. Bickerstaff, a bearded, dignified

gentleman, asked the boarding party, 'What do you intend to do?'

He was told, but he did not like it. However, he was allowed to fetch his golf clubs and tennis racquet before his crew was ordered off. The poor man watched his big command sink from the bridge of the *Emden*.

Markomannia and *Pontoporos*—dubbed 'junkmen', were already becoming crowded with the crews, and some passengers from the day's four prizes. It was an experience for him, since, from all the reports of German raiders, he half expected swashbucklers on a frowsy pirate ship.

When served tea and invited to the afternoon concert of the ship's band, he was dumbfounded, but appreciative. The musicians included selections such as 'That Was in Schöneberg in the Lovely Month of May.' He visibly stiffened when the concert ended with 'Watch on the Rhine.'

Before midnight, as the cruiser was steaming northward towards Calcutta, in the Bay of Bengal, lights were sighted ahead. The job of a raider in darkness was very dangerous, von Müller was well aware. Too late one may discover the 'old freighter' is a battle cruiser with six-inch guns.

On the other hand, the commander may decide it is an enemy warship, open fire and perhaps sink it with heavy loss of life only to discover it was a neutral vessel. And how could von Müller explain that to Berlin and Berlin in turn to the United States, or South America?

Von Müller pushed in close to this latest stranger, then turned on the huge searchlights on the *Emden*'s foremast. It was a freighter.

'Who are you, where bound?'

'*Killin*, out of Glasgow. Bound from Calcutta for England with 6,000 tons of coal,' came the reply, co-operatively.

In the rough seas, Captain J. K. Wilson, of the *Killin*, was transferred on to the *Emden*, and his crew on the *Pontoporos*. Now Captain Bickerstaff had company. The *Killin* was an old and slow ship, and there was also more of the soft, miserable Indian coal aboard the *Pontoporos* than needed. However, a prize crew went aboard her.

Now, the *Markomannia*, *Pontoporos* and *Killin* were trailing astern, like Nubian slaves in the Egypt of the Pharaohs. *Emden* was slowed down to eight knots, which meant she would have to abandon all three at the slightest sign of serious trouble—the materializing of the *Minotaur*, for example. The wireless man still was receiving her intermittent messages, and at times it appeared she was paralleling the *Emden*'s course up the Bay of Bengal.

In the morning, something happened to increase *Emden*'s precarious position. A wallowing ship identified herself as the *Loredano*, out of Venice, and a neutral. The boarding party took one quick look at the dirtiness of her decks, and crew, to confirm that she was indeed an old Italian tramp.

'Proceed, *Loredano*,' von Müller instructed, adding, 'Keep silent as to *Emden*.'

She left a trail of smoke as she sloshed slowly over the southern horizon. Within an hour after she had disappeared, her morse-code warning was heard:

'Don't leave harbour—*Emden* in vicinity!'

The *Loredano*'s alarm together with the slow 'convoy' speed forced upon him by the presence of the *Pontoporos*, *Killin* and his own *Markomannia* had made von Müller's position increasingly precarious. He could easily be bottled up in the narrow head of the Bay of Bengal from which there was no exit save the turgid mouth of the dirty Hooghly River.

For two nights, because of these considerations, he deliberately passed opportunities to investigate possible prizes. Then, late on September 12th, in a choppy sea, he saw a medium-sized vessel making directly for the *Emden*.

Searchlights were played on the stranger as von Müller blew his siren for her to halt. She obeyed.

This time he sent his youngest officer, with a small party, to board her. A tall, thin, serious-faced man, in oilskins, was waiting at the gangway.

'I'm Captain Thomas Robinson,' he identified himself. 'This is the *Kabinga*, 4,657 tons, of the Ellerman and Bucknell Steamship Co., of London. We are bound from Calcutta for New York, under charter by an American firm, via Bombay, Port Said and the Mediterranean. The cargo is mostly jute, together with some assorted merchandise—neutral cargo, of course, since it is all consigned to the United States,' He paused. 'There are also some Americans in my crew.'

The information was speedily relayed by blinker back to von Müller. The German officer was in for further surprise when he walked with the master of the *Kabinga* to his cabin.

Inside the teakwood-panelled cabin was a woman, about thirty-five years old, clad in nightgown and shawl.

Her hair was mussed as though she had been asleep and awakened suddenly. She had been crying.

Suddenly she ran over to the German and clutched the lapels of his half-torn oilskins, in an imploring gesture.

'Oh, please, don't kill us,' she gasped. 'Please!'

Now, the German officer noticed a little boy, right behind the woman, holding on to her nightdress and whimpering. He stole quick, frightened glances at the intruder.

'It's all right, Tom,' the Captain said, putting his hand on the child's head. 'He won't hurt you.' Then he introduced his wife, and young Tom.

When Mrs. Robinson had recovered her composure and had been persuaded to sit on the divan, her feeling of relief was speedily manifest.

'You have been at sea a long time,' she mentioned, noticing the frayed aspects of the German's uniform. 'And you must need tobacco, cigarettes. . . .' She looked at her husband. 'Tom, we have an extra supply. . . .'

The *Kabinga*'s master nodded, but before he could reply, the German signalman entered the quarters. He whispered to his officer, who then turned to Robinson.

'Captain von Müller,' he explained, 'would like your ship to join us—temporarily.'

Captain Robinson was not surprised.

'You will fall astern with three other merchant ships, the *Markomannia*, *Killin* and *Pontoporos*. Perhaps you have encountered the *Killin* before? Perhaps you know Captain Wilson . . . ?'

The merchant skipper nodded, then asked if he could keep his revolver.

'You may,' the *Emden*'s officer smiled. 'But you will

have no use for it. As a matter of fact, you are safer with us than in a port like Liverpool.' He frowned at the memory of a visit there when a cadet, the squalid sooty slums of Bootle, the brawling shipfitters' bars of dingy Birkenhead.

The German spent the night aboard. A cot had been fixed for him in the wireless shack. He had no fears now that Captain Robinson would try to escape this convoy of four merchant ships or send a message from some hidden transmitter. They were gentlemen for the most part, these English officers, merchant or naval . . . and that made him wonder, as he sometimes had in the past, why two proud nations, with seemingly the same civilized standards, were now bent on mutual destruction.

But tonight, the young German had other thoughts. Perhaps the paper, in the form of wireless blanks, perhaps the sight of a woman and a child, or simply loneliness' own intoxicant—whatever the motivation, he wanted to write his sweetheart.

'Dear Ilse,' he started, then crossed it out. 'Sweetheart . . .' He cancelled that, too.

My darling,
   The weeks have fled like autumn leaves. Has it been months since I said good-bye to you at Wilhelmshaven, or eternity? Dearest one, I lie awake in the depths of night time, and try to believe you are here, beside me. . . .

The waxy, nostalgic smell of a panelled room was somehow like home. The *Kabinga's* pistons wheezed and pulsed far below. Tom cried out as he turned in his sleep. . . .

Yet his reactions were not unique. Other officers and sailors, German and English, that night dreamed of home and those they loved, whether or not they wrote letters.

They remembered music, such as the tinny strains from the Löwenbräukeller in Munich of *'Ach wie ist's möglich, dan'*, or the more light-hearted *'S'ist mir alles eins, 's'ist mir alles eins* . . .*'*

. . . or walking arm-in-arm in Hagenbecks Tierpark in Hamburg, tossing peanuts to the lazy old elephants as the bands, always the bands, blared *'Die Lorelei'* . . . or of the bands in Victoria Park playing 'Tipperary'.

. . . or simply the natural symphony the sighing which many trees make in the Black Forest, or in the Bavarian Alps surrounding Garmisch, or in the Harz mountains, near Blankenburg, familiar to a captain named von Müller, for one . . . the villages of Dorset, familiar to a captain named Robinson, for one.

. . . or the more humble, simple sounds of home in any land and of a sleeping city, of an attic stairway creaking its rasping, intimate lullaby, the dripping tap, the tick-tock from a scarcely-noticed clock, the indefinable whisperings of an old structure, and outside the thud of infrequent footsteps, perhaps a policeman—a Bobby in London, a Polizist in Berlin—the banging of trams, the piping of a train whistle, the bark of a dog.

At sea, in an infinity of water, there were none of these familiar and blandishing nuances save out of the comforting cushion of memory.

CHAPTER 6

AS soon as it was light the next morning, Sunday, the *Kabinga* was ordered to one side of the convoy. Then the crack-crack of the *Emden*'s guns drilled the silence of a new day at sea.

The *Killin* was the target. No more Indian coal was needed.

Last night's terror returned to the eyes of Mrs. Robinson as she watched beside her husband on the bridge.

'Will we be next?' she asked, looking at Tommy who was holding his ears against the noise.

Jagged holes were gashed in the *Killin*. She surged from side to side, wounded. Quickly she assumed a steep list to port, almost fifty degrees, as her bow plunged lower.

All were silent now on the bridge of the *Kabinga*. Mrs. Robinson continued to watch in semi-fascinated dread.

With a hissing of steam and belching of black smoke, the *Killin* went under, barely lifting her stern out of water in her haste to have her own execution over. As a whitish-greenish mound of water frothed where she had disappeared, a cutter put out from the *Emden*, and steamed toward the *Kabinga*.

Captain Robinson figured the *Kabinga* would be next. He asked the young German officer, but the latter did not know.

E   [65]

'You better pack up,' he said to his wife, then told his first officers: 'Stand by, we will probably be abandoning. Pass the word!'

When the cutter puffed alongside, none of the English sailors was quite prepared to see Captain von Müller himself. Immaculate in a fresh uniform, he came aboard the freighter with a manner of casual friendliness.

'It's an honour to be on your ship,' he said in fluent English to Captain Robinson, saluting. 'I'm sorry we have had to stop you.' He paused to tip his hat to Mrs. Robinson. 'I think we have met somewhere, Mr. Robinson? Samoa, perhaps? Well, no matter. I want to assure your wife that the Germans wish to be friends with the English people. This war has been forced upon us, and we regret it as much as you.' There was a faint nervous twitch around his eyes. 'Mrs. Robinson, I give you the *Kabinga*.' He turned to her husband. 'You may inform your owners that as far as they are concerned officially the *Kabinga* has been seized and sunk.'

Von Müller saluted, and started down the ladder for his cutter, leaving written instructions for his assistant to read.

'Captain Robinson,' von Müller's young officer said, 'about three hundred passengers will come aboard in the next half hour, from our other ships. We will escort you to the mouth of the Hooghly River and there leave you. But be careful of the approaches to the Hooghly; buoys have been removed, lightships and pilot vessels are off station. We know that from Calcutta radio.'

The Robinsons waved from the bridge as the launch drew off. She held up her little boy's hand and he, too, waved. Then, the waters suddenly rang with an incredible sound:

'Hurrah. . . . !' A pause, then 'hurrah!' and a final 'hurrah!'

The *Kabinga's* thankful crew had given a lusty three cheers.

Von Müller was looking away, at the *Emden*. He would not turn to face his officers until they were climbing back up the gangway to the cruiser.

All that bright Sunday morning *Emden* steamed up the coast of India, towards the Hooghly River, the *Pontoporos* and the *Markomannia* astern, the *Kabinga* just ahead with Captain Bickerstaff, Captain Wilson and the other crews and passengers aboard. Church was conducted on the poop deck. Von Müller read the prayers and the band accompanied as the crew sang:

> O God, our help in ages past,
> Our hope for years to come,
> Our shelter from the stormy blast,
> And our eternal home. . . .

As the sailors concluded, there were tears pouring down several beard-stubbled cheeks.

> Be Thou our guard
> While troubles last,
> And our eternal home. . . .

Within seventy-five miles of the Sandheads, outside of the Hooghly, the *Emden* turned southward again, after signalling to the *Kabinga*, even as Admiral von Spee had signalled weeks ago off Pagan Island:

'*Auf Wiedersehen*!'

Emden was trapped in a corner of the Bay of Bengal. The *Hampshire* or the *Minotaur* could easily bottle her up here and blast the cruiser to bits. Von Müller lost no time in turning back towards the wide mouth of the bay, roughly between the Nicobar Islands and Ceylon.

By late evening a wireless message was intercepted from the *Kabinga*, calling for a pilot close to the Sandheads.

Nothing was intercepted from the *Kabinga* to indicate she was broadcasting *Emden*'s position.

In the morning the *Clan Matheson* was overtaken. She stopped without murmur, as though she had half expected the German cruiser. She was a 4,700-tonner, Glasgow registry, bound from Calcutta.

Von Muecke this time took a party aboard and met Captain W. Harris.

'We're on our way to Colombo,' he reported, 'to pick up troops for France. But,' he shook his head gravely, 'I'm sorry you caught us. I wonder how you knew we were here. . . .'

The *Emden*'s first officer understood his regret, and the problem it posed when he went below. Tied and bedded in a row of stalls were a pair of thoroughbred racehorses.

'They are fresh from the Calcutta Sweepstakes,' Captain Harris explained, with a warm look in his eyes. 'We also have a cargo of Rolls Royces and typewriters.' He shook his head again. The horses whinnied and stomped their feet, nervously.

There seemed but one humane thing to do. Von

Muecke took his Luger from its holster. He sent a bullet crashing through the skulls of the two animals. They fell to their stall floors and died. They stared open-eyed, as their heads slumped, and the blood trickled in a matted stream from the holes the automatic had drilled.

'War is waste,' Captain Harris remarked as the men returned to his cabin. Von Muecke accepted his offer of brandy.

Two hours later, the *Clan Matheson*, of Glasgow, slipped beneath the waters of the Bay of Bengal. But the memory of the horses, the smell of the stalls below decks, the red streamlets of blood could not be erased as quickly as the ship.

In the night the lights of another ship were spotted. As the *Emden* took after her, lights were extinguished. She disappeared in a rain squall driving in from Burma, immediately to the east.

Through the early pre-dawn hours, von Müller doggedly hunted for that vessel. Shapes materialized out of the rain, only to dissolve again. It was, truly, a ghost ship.

As morning broke, von Müller saw how far off-course he had sailed. The outlines of pagodas were visible not far off the port bow. *Emden* was coming in fast for the Burma coast.

'Hard a-starboard!' The helmsman spun the wheel, and the cruiser steamed westward again. The waters were full of sandbars.

Later in the day, von Müller rejoined the *Markomannia* and *Pontoporos* and set a south-west course. The following morning he overhauled the *Doore*, a small freighter of

Norwegian registry, bound for Rangoon. Von Müller asked if she would take the crew of the *Clan Matheson*.

'Yes,' the *Doore* blinked back, 'at the usual passage rates.'

A neutral vessel would expect compensation. Von Müller would sign vouchers, reimbursable at any German Admiralty office. The *Doore* decided the vouchers were acceptable.

Before Captain Harris left, he shook hands with von Müller.

'You have been courteous,' the Englishman said flatly, 'but how long do you think you can keep this up, in waters controlled by our Navy?'

'I rather expect to be captured eventually,' von Müller answered frankly. 'But we want to make a good run for it. You can hardly blame us.'

That night the truth of Captain Harris' assertion was emphasized. The *Hampshire* was heard conversing with a shore station and with the *Minotaur*. From their transmission it was evident that they were close by, searching for the *Emden*, and the *Emden* alone.

'We have to get out,' von Müller said. 'We've been up in the Bay of Bengal too long. No merchant ships will venture out now. We must plan a new phase of operations.'

All that night, von Müller, his first officer, his navigation officer and gunnery officer sat up and pondered.

The sultry Indian winds whistled across masts and funnels and the *Emden* rolled. Wireless traffic continued heavy, and once again, a shore operator tapped:

'Where are you, *Emden*?' then added, 'you bloody rascal!'

Emden patrolled two days off Rangoon, without results. Von Müller was committed to alter his avowed tactics, which were to war exclusively on merchant shipping. It reflected a certain impatience which had grown, if subtly, within him. The strain, the loneliness of his mission was having an effect on his entire emotional complex. He had to keep moving and on the offensive, even though he well knew that these very qualities could ultimately lead but to the doom of his command.

He determined on a bombardment of the sprawling city of Madras, home to one and a half million persons, a major seaport on India's south-east coast.

Principal targets would be the fat cluster of oil tanks on the harbour's edge. In addition to physical destruction of material essential to Britain's war effort, the raid would, von Müller calculated, have a shattering effect on enemy morale, and perhaps send additional shipping scurrying for port. He would then speed to a new area and attack without warning.

Markomannia and *Pontoporos* would rendezvous within a week at a spot in the Bay of Bengal north-west of the Nicobar Islands. The *Markomannia* would steam half a day ahead of the *Pontoporos* and fly the Brazilian flag, 'heading in ballast for Hong Kong'. Flying the Greek flag, with her prize crew in command, the *Pontoporos* was supposedly on her original voyage, 'delayed by engine trouble'.

The two freighters steamed off to the East, and no one on board the *Emden* was at all certain if he would ever see them again.

Meanwhile, on September 21st, final preparations

were made for von Müller's bold assault. In the surgery,
there was quiet but thorough activity. Steel instruments
were polished until they gleamed like gold and silver
under the cabin's strong lights. Bandages were rolled
neatly and lined up inside sterile glass cabinets. Against
the wall, stretchers were in readiness, and on the deck,
many jars of vaseline and other jellies: for burns.

Von Müller considered the defences of Madras very
strong.

The next afternoon, and early evening, as the cruiser
boiled across seas whipped by a howling south-west
monsoon, the band musicians sought to bolster morale.
They played 'Deutschland uber Alles', 'Wir fahren nach
England', 'Die Wacht am Rhein', all the stirring songs.

News from the wireless also stimulated every man on
board. Kapitänleutnant Otto Weddigen, in the Submarine U-9, had just torpedoed and sunk the British
cruisers Cressy, Aboukir and Hogue in a fantastically daring
attack off the Hook of Holland. Cheers went up and
the Unterseebooten service was toasted, in water, all
around.

This was followed by a bulletin from Reuter. The
Emden, it advised, had been sunk off the Maldive Islands
in a running gun fight with the Hampshire.

Shortly after 8 p.m., as the crew waited, in clean
clothes, at battle stations, Madras Light was picked up.
One of the most unusual lighthouses in the world. It is
mounted 160 feet high on the very dome of the Law
Courts buildings. The Emden was twenty miles east of
Madras when the look-out first saw it blinking, in group
flashes of two every thirty seconds.

The spray and the rain dashed into the crew's faces

as the *Emden* continued through the offshore chop. It was warm, and soupy. The beacon from the Law Courts tower vanished for several minutes at a time as the scudding clouds came across in cottony wads, then lifted again.

On the bridge, officers were doing a delicate job of navigation, to avoid the sandbars.

Soon, dark shapes on the water began sweeping at the cruiser, and then passing, just as mysteriously, perhaps fishing dhows and sampans, or unlighted channel buoys.

Just before nine o'clock, the blacked-out raider was hauling close to Madras. This was indicated by the increased height and brilliance of the lighthouse, and the reddish glow against the clouds from other buildings of the vast city. Maps of Madras showed von Müller was approaching its northern reaches. Located there were the storage tanks of oil companies, behind them the huge native quarter, Georgetown, and two miles further inland along Konnur Road, suburban Vepery.

On the immediate southern fringe of the oil tanks was located Central Railways station and old Fort St. George, with barracks and government offices. All were legitimate targets should shells land on them, though it was not known whether Fort St. George was now part of the harbour defences.

At a range of less than two miles, as the silhouettes of temples and their minarets were added to the dim outline of Madras, von Müller gave the order to train on target. It should be dead ahead. And in another second it was —the oil tank area. The searchlights were helpfully illuminating them. They were painted white, with ornamental stripes of red!

'Fire!'

The *Emden*'s broadside crashed towards Madras, wham-wham-wham!

In seconds a huge white flash on shore and a torrent of bluish, yellow flames billowing upward.

Another broadside. The flames leaped higher . . . and a smaller flaring between the *Emden* and the shore . . . as though a hit on a ship at anchorage.

The *Emden* wheeled, paralleling the coast, no more than 2,000 yards off . . . suddenly her running lights flashed on, searchlights played on the water from fore and aft masts, while lights blazed from open ports. It was an intentional ruse on the part of von Müller to confuse the defences into thinking this was a merchant ship, while the unknown attacker was possibly speeding, blacked-out, along some other area of the long waterfront.

Emden plunged through the darkness. The flames illuminated the land, bringing Madras into reddish-shadowy focus like some wild canvas. The low-hanging clouds still haloed the temple spires.

Then, blinking from the forts, or from a vessel just off the sandflats:

'Who are you? Who are you? Who are you?'

Rapidly the code challenge was spelled out, again and again.

The raider's answer:

'Fire!'

A crashing salvo of all port guns, heavy calibre and machine guns. Several rounds answered, stabs of light, like angry fireflies. One shell whined high overhead.

The blinker challenge stopped as abruptly as it had

started. The cruiser's lights were extinguished. *Emden* was swallowed up again in the protective folds of the stormy tropical night.

The fort's fire dwindled, ceased altogether.

Emden raced eastward across the Bay of Bengal, bumping over the choppy waters like a car on a rutted road, leaving wounded Madras far astern. A westerly wind blew the flames toward the sea, sparing the capital of Madras State from more serious incineration.

Within an hour the wireless operator intercepted a message from the *Hampshire*: it was steaming, from the north, hard for Madras.

The clarity of the signals indicated it was only a few miles away. Von Müller swung the helm. *Emden* leaned into her turn as course was changed to the southeast.

Later in the night, nearly ninety miles away, the burning oils tanks glared red on the horizon. And before morning, wireless reports offered details of the damage.

At least two tanks of the Burma Oil Co. Ltd., set on fire, one watchman and a town constable killed . . . buildings damaged including a beach bungalow belonging to the Port Trust . . . several shells, allegedly, had fallen on suburban Vepery, Shoolay and the native quarter, Georgetown, causing panic . . . eight officers had been injured on the British India Steam Navigation Co., ship *Chupra*, caught in the line of fire. . . .

And meanwhile, in London, the Admiralty announced that the British cruiser *Cumberland* had captured off the Cameroons, in West Africa, the Hamburg-America liner *Arnfried*, the *Max Brock*, *Kenapa*, *Henrietta Woermann* and

[75]

six other merchant steamers of German registry, 'all in good order and most contained general cargoes and considerable quantities of coal'.

There was a rumour that von Kluck was trapped in France, his army about to be annihilated.

Somehow, von Kluck was not aware of this, and his army on the Western Front, as von Hindenburg's on the Eastern—'juggernauts', newspapers kept labelling them—continued to hammer out what seemed to the world like an ultimate German victory.

CHAPTER 7

FOR several days the raider cruised in circles. No ruse must be overlooked to deceive the enemy and to keep him expending his energy on fruitless quests.

Nonetheless, the situation was becoming more grave. It was reflected in the little mannerisms of von Müller. He began, for example, to smoke more, though in the past there were times when he was not known to smoke at all. The indication of a welling nervousness within him was especially apparent to officers from whom he borrowed cigarettes.

While he always made an effort to eat in the mess with his officers, he began to shorten these periods so that he could get back to the domain which claimed by far the majority of his waking hours—his navigation bridge.

There he would walk slowly back and forth, sometimes pausing to ask the familiar question of his navigation officer:

'Nothing new, Mr. Gropius?'

And more often than not, the reply:

'Nothing new, sir.'

And if it were daytime, von Müller would then light up a cigarette and blow the smoke thoughtfully into the wind, perhaps momentarily resting his elbows on the railing. His eyes were focused on the horizon, where sea and sky almost melted together, watching, always watching—and waiting.

Between meals, von Müller took to nibbling snacks, perhaps compulsively, in the little pantry adjoining his own cabin.

He laughed infrequently. His staff came to think of him as a grave and pensive man. The more perceptive could recognize in him the qualities, or the curse, of a driven man—but what those forces were that drove him no one could say.

The night after the Madras attack, he called his senior officers together.

'There are at least sixteen major enemy warships after us,' he announced. 'They include the *Hampshire*, as you are well aware, the *Minotaur*, *Weymouth*, *Gloucester*, *Yarmouth* . . . commanded by a friend, Henry Cochrane . . . the auxiliary cruisers, *Empress of Russia* and *Empress of Asia*. Somewhat farther away are the Australian cruisers *Sydney*, *Melbourne*, the French cruiser *Montcalm*, the Japanese vessels *Ibuki*, *Yakagi* and *Chikuna*, the Russian *Askold*. . . .'

The *Emden* continued her evasive tactics. The sea was strangely empty of shipping, in testimony to the fame the little cruiser had evoked for her prowess. Britain's freighters were in port, von Müller concluded, her lifeline had been severed.

Then, on the night of September 26th, von Müller steamed within blinker distance of Colombo. It was not only bold, it was arrogant, and there was a deep, quiet humour in von Müller's expression as he watched for enemy gunboats.

These tactics also hinted at a certain disdain for the

enemy's fleet in Eastern waters, even though von Müller had just briefed his officers on its overwhelming might.

Searchlights played across the skies, illuminating the harbour entrance. Watch officers, through binoculars, could trace the outlines of the city itself. Von Müller, who knew Colombo well, recalled the buffalo steaks in the Grand Oriental Hotel, the gin and quinine, the ginger beer, the crooked streets as crowded with rickshaws as Hong Kong itself, the orange trees growing casually as weeds in back yards, the multi-coloured, dazzling vegetation . . . it was a lush parcel of earth in no way cousin to Blankenburg, but he had a feeling for it just the same.

As the diminutive *Emden* bore down on the city, some of her sailors could swear their captain planned to drive right into the breakwater and boldly drop anchor beside, perhaps, the *Hampshire*. They would not have put it entirely past this man of quiet daring.

Searchlights continued to crisscross ahead as though the *Emden* had already been observed and a course were being lighted to help the cruiser navigate in.

Then white lights, bobbing—a pilot vessel? There was a hasty conference on the bridge whether, if pilot it were, he should be brought aboard and forced to steer *Emden* in through Colombo's minefields. The gunners would blast every enemy warship found in the sanctuary, and then the *Emden* would head out again as fast as she could go, while the British wondered what had hit them.

In a moment, von Müller had overhauled the lights. They blazed on the stern, not of a pilot vessel but a freighter of some 3,000 tons.

'Who are you?' von Müller blinked. When it did not answer, he added:

'Stop at once!'

The ship still ignored the command, but was so close to Colombo, von Müller dared not fire a warning shot, or even a rocket. Instead he took a chance almost as great. He ordered a lengthy message to be flashed to the freighter:

'This is *Emden*. Reverse your engines immediately or we will blow you to pieces!'

Emden was close enough for her signals to be easily picked up by a sharp-eyed lookout at the naval control station on Colombo breakwater. It was as though an enemy warship were capturing an American coastal freighter off Fire Island, at the sea approaches to New York City, or a British frigate in the Thames Estuary.

It was unthinkable. But it happened. No one detected the *Emden*'s open insolence in Britain's colonial backyard.

Now a thrashing of black water as the stranger reversed engines. Then, the reply, winking excitedly through the night:

'We are *Tymeric*. British registry.'

Von Müller knew she was too close in shore to sink her. His best boarding crew would have to scramble up her sides and shepherd her along.

The operation was done in an incredibly short time. Lauterbach, chosen to command this prize crew, was not greeted warmly.

'You damned Germans!' raged the master of the *Tymeric*. 'You're always on our track. Why can't you leave us alone?' He was short, middle-aged, grizzled and weather-beaten.

'You stop that talk,' Lauterbach replied. 'This is not a personal affair. Don't you understand war?'

Grudgingly, and further persuaded by the ugly snouts of two Maxim guns held by the boarding party, the merchant captain brought out his papers. *Tymeric*, they showed, was fat with a full cargo of rum and sugar.

Emden blinked again.

'Follow me!' Already her stern light was swinging around as von Müller set course for the Arabian Sea . . . 250, 255, 260, 265, 270 degrees . . . due west her compass read as her pistons strained to carry her beyond this sleeping lair of the Royal Navy.

Lauterbach's problems were far from ended. He heard the *Tymeric's* captain whispering hurriedly to his chief engineer, using long English words under an erroneous assumption the German officer would not understand. But Lauterbach did. They would feign engine trouble, then lag behind until a British patrol boat might come to their rescue.

Lauterbach did not consider this proper talk. He felt a certain personal hurt that the English captain would connive to save his own ship. He reacted quickly, by sending a demolition team below while his signalmen blinked towards the *Emden*, now starting to pull away from the freighter, like a greyhound stretching into stride.

'Something is wrong. Request permission to sink *Tymeric* immediately!'

The request was granted.

'I will give you five minutes to abandon,' Lauterbach said peremptorily to the *Tymeric*'s master.

'But the naval authorities in Colombo assured us these waters were perfectly safe,' the latter protested.

Lauterbach looked at him.

Sea valves were opened, fuses set. Within ten minutes all hands were off the doomed ship, and five minutes later were coming aboard the *Emden*. It was decided to post an armed guard outside the mine gear locker where the master and his chief engineer were temporarily imprisoned.

The freighter was still in sight when there was a flash, a dull 'boom!' and several thousand tons of rum and sugar started for the bottom of the Arabian Sea.

None of Ceylon's defence forces had as yet put out to challenge these operations of the *Emden*.

Lauterbach had carried a number of Bombay, Calcutta and Colombo newspapers with him from the freighter. The fame of the slim little raider was spreading beyond all proportion to her size, or even her armament. On the front page of one paper was an advertisement proclaiming:

'Our soap is so good that even the *Emden* took it from the *Indus* and used it.'

Brief editorial comment lauded von Müller's 'fair play' and concluded that he must be a 'real sportsman'.

One article datelined 'New Delhi (delayed by censor), September 17th', commenced:

'No alarm is felt here at the recent capture of British ships by the German cruiser *Emden*, as she is being pursued by British cruisers.'

Another one in the same paper blandly reported that

all trade routes to Penang had been closed for the past ten days and shipping in the Bay of Bengal was almost paralyzed. Pondicherry, just below Madras, had been on an alert ever since the *Emden*'s bombardment of her big neighbour up the coast. There was an oblique reference to natives riding inland atop train coaches.

The *Kabinga* had arrived in Calcutta safely, and Captain Robinson had reported the *Emden*'s treatment as most courteous—an opinion with which none of the some three hundred other prisoners disagreed.

George Read, second officer of the *Indus*, gave an interview claiming 'The marksmanship of the German gunners was poor. It took dozens of shots to sink the *Indus*.'

Anglo-French forces had invaded the Cameroons, Peronne had been recaptured by the Entente, and a Japanese squadron had commenced a day and night bombardment of Tsingtao, using aeroplanes to spot the fire. German planes were fighting them off.

Between the time of the sinking of the *Tymeric* and the end of September, four other Allied ships were seized by the *Emden*. Area of operations was a wide one, extending from Rangoon down the Bay of Bengal to the Nicobar Islands where the *Markomannia* and *Pontoporos* re-joined convoy.

The *King Lud* was as rat-ridden an old coaster as ever sailed the Seven Seas. It was considered by von Müller a public service to send her to the bottom, even if her Captain Harris might have thought otherwise. There was the *Foyle*, a new, larger and ratless ship, also the *Buresk*. The *Buresk* was a find, loaded with 7,000 tons of high-grade Cardiff coal. She joined the *Markomannia* and *Pontoporos*, her voyage to Hong Kong indefinitely interrupted.

By now, interrogation of merchant masters had settled to routine. They knew in a general way the location of other ships that had left port at about the same time as they. For that reason they usually assumed von Müller knew, too.

'Have you seen ship X?' they would ask.

'No,' von Müller would reply, disarmingly.

'Why, that's strange, she's only half a day ahead of me,' or 'less than a day behind.'

With that information, the *Emden* would steam off and shortly find ship X.

One captain unwittingly tipped his hand by asking, 'How did you learn of the new and secret course laid out for merchantmen by the Admiralty?'

Von Müller hadn't, until then.

The *Ribera* proved a source of other information. Its captain, J. Isdale, was co-operative and genial.

'I don't think you'll find many more steamers in the Indian Ocean now,' Captain Isdale volunteered. 'The British are keeping vessels in harbour because of fear of the *Emden*. Insurance rates have gone so high it's almost impractical to take out any, don't you know?' He added he'd seen the cruiser *Königsberg* in the Indian Ocean, though he was unable to say how he missed being captured.

Now there were too many crews from the captured ships, depleting the larders of the *Markomannia* and *Pontoporos*. A slow freighter from Glasgow, the *Gryfevale*, in ballast, steamed over the horizon on October 1st and solved the problem. The two hundred or so of prisoners of war were packed on board her.

There was temporary trouble while the prisoners were being billeted in the *Gryfevale*. Many had been allowed to bring whisky with them. Parties roared prematurely into boisterous, fighting existence. Blood was drawn as fists and broken bottles flew.

Von Müller was glad when the freighter was ready to be sped on her way and his boarding party recalled to the church-like atmosphere, by comparison, of the *Emden*. A special course was given her Captain, J. W. Steel, to Cochin, Indo-China, with the warning that if he strayed off, safe passage would *not* be assured.

Next morning, a wireless message from her, as she stood off Cochin awaiting a pilot, indicated she had not strayed, but been obedient to the letter.

September had almost run out, this September of 1914, the year something called 'modern war' was born. And, in between the massive news of human avalanches engulfing the European continent and ending an era, there was yet room for dispatches like this, in the *New York Times*:

EMDEN SINKS MORE SHIPS

FOUR BRITISH STEAMERS IN INDIAN OCEAN DESTROYED BY GERMAN CRUISER

London, September 29th: Through the official News Bureau, the Admiralty to-day announced that the German cruiser *Emden* in the last few days had captured and sunk in the Indian Ocean 4 British

[85]

steamers—the *Tymeric*, *King Lud*, *Ribera* and *Foyle* and had captured the collier *Buresk*. The captured crews were transferred to the steamer *Gryfevale* which also had been captured but which was released to take the crews to Colombo, Ceylon, where they arrived this morning.

An official statement issued September 20th told of the capture by the *Emden* of 6 British steamers in the Bay of Bengal and the sinking of 5 of them. The steamers were the *Indus*, *Lovat*, *Killin*, *Diplomat*, *Trabboch* and *Kabinga*.

After creating havoc among British shipping at Calcutta the *Emden* went to Rangoon. She was reported recently at Madras where she conducted a brief bombardment of that port, and later at Pondicherry.

September gave way to October. But, to the crew of the *Emden*, it was not the October they knew in the homeland, the harvest-month of Oktoberfest, smell of roasting chestnuts, sound of music in beer halls, the proximity of gentleness, of softness, of—women. To Karl von Müller, Blankenburg, its blandishing autumnal breezes and all they bespoke or hinted was at least a million miles and another existence removed.

Reality was the *Emden*, was the searing, equatorial vastness of the Indian Ocean. Reality was the loneliness, hunger and seeking, always seeking, empty primitive seeking, with no time even to ask a question in the depths of isolation—why? where?

Yet there were occasional flickerings of relief from tension which otherwise would have been unbearable, and even subtle shadings of humour. Some were in the form of the *Emden* legends which Captain N. Leslie, for one, of the *Clan Grant*, had passed on to his captors.

One legend, accepted ashore with the weight of fact, concerned a radio request for coal . . . and a warship using the call letters of a British cruiser.

This cruiser, according to the report, had been chasing the *Emden* for six weeks up and down the Indian Ocean. Rather than allow the trail to grow cold, the Britisher had made kindling of furniture, hatch shorings and wall panellings to feed her hungry furnaces once bunkers were exhausted of coal. When virtually a bare shell, she was forced to refuel. Only 200 miles off the south-west Indian coast, she would dash in, bunker up and dash out again after the fleeing *Emden*.

Indian authorities received the urgent request. Clerks hurried to under-officials and under-officials to higher officials and higher officials to the commissioner-expeditor himself for military supplies. Within an hour, long goods trains were being loaded with coal.

All passenger traffic was shunted to sidings as freights whistled along the coast to the secret port where the fuel-starved cruiser was due to put in. Oddly enough, nothing was said about food for the crew. The inescapable assumption was that they were fishing, or perhaps practising cannibalism, rather than risk letting the *Emden* give them the slip.

On schedule, the trains rolled into the yards. Gangs of native labourers, hastily recruited, toiled all night to pile mountains of coal on the dock, ready to load as soon as the English cruiser arrived.

Finally all was ready. But, no cruiser—nor any further word from her.

The officials and the native leaders waited. They bided time a day, a second day, and a third. The commissioner-expeditor for military supplies grew irked and questioned the officials who reported to him, they in turn criticized the under-officials until finally the clerks at the very bottom of officialdom who had transcribed the original request from the wireless were rebuked vehemently.

The Royal Navy could draw one conclusion. The wily old *Emden* herself had sent that message. But how she had coded it in the Admiralty's own secret gibberish was a mystery, careful as everyone was in the Royal Navy with matters like Royal code books.

Von Müller was flattered that such skill and intelligence had been attributed to him. Other stories had him doing so many things at so many widely separated points that his *Emden* must be a whole squadron of cruisers. In the same night, legend had it, the *Emden* would be pretending she was a pilot vessel at the mouth of the Hooghly to lure freighters into the Bay, while also warped to a dock in Colombo, disguised as a Russian cruiser. Her officers and crew disported themselves in the city.

Von Müller, it was also rumoured, had been made an honorary member of Calcutta's principal club.

And so they went. Throughout all these stories, one fact filtered through: the respect enemies, and neutrals as well, had for the *Emden* and for the chivalrous conduct of von Müller.

The *Clan Grant*, as a matter of fact, had been more than

a source of *Emden* legends. Her cavernous holds were
rich with cargo from England: from cigarettes and
crockery, to oil and live cattle. Much of it was unloaded leisurely and stored aboard the *Emden* as the *Clan
Grant* kept in company with her captor for several days
before she was destroyed.

Somehow, in the process, Professor Patrick Geddes, of
the Botany Department, University College, Dundee,
had lost what he called his life's work. It consisted of
models, charts, maps and diagrams in addition to hundreds of thousands of words on his history of the evolu-
tion of civic life.

Ever afterwards, the name *Emden* was anathema to the
professor from Scotland.

North of the Nicobar Islands, one night, the powerful
Hampshire again passed by. Von Müller heard her
wireless transmission, saw her lights. He watched, and
wondered.

A message was intercepted from the *Minotaur*. She
was patrolling east of the Maldive Islands, on the hunch
the *Emden* might be in those westerly waters. The
Yarmouth was less garrulous, but there was reason to
suspect she was waiting somewhere to the south, perhaps
between Diego Garcia and the Cocos Islands. The
Ibuki should be lurking off Sumatra, blocking an exit to
the east.

The ring was being drawn around the *Emden*.

By now the *Emden* was heavy with rust and barnacles.
Something had to be done. Von Müller wanted a quiet
forgotten island where he could make repairs and
repaint as best he could. And Diego Garcia, a coral
atoll governed by the British, south of Mauritius

and 420 miles above the Equator, appeared to be ideal.

Emden cut west across the Bay of Bengal, past the Maldive Islands. On October 9th, she probed through the narrow, coral-reef channel into the pin-point which was Diego Garcia. There a couple of hundred inhabitants bartered coconut oil, copra, tortoise shell, coral and fish as a livelihood—commodities which were of little use in the raider's grim demands for existence.

The anchor chain had scarcely stopped clanking through the hawse-pipe when a man put out in a small canoe. Quite a sight in his wide-brimmed palm frond hat, tattered white shirt and bare feet, he was a Creole and perhaps seventy years old. This was a strange situation and no one was quite sure how to handle it.

'Morning chaps,' he rasped pleasantly.

He carried a basket of vegetables and eggs, also a slatted crate of coconut crabs, known as a real delicacy.

'It's so nice of a German ship to call at our little island,' he continued. 'The last one was—let me see, now, was it '89?—when your frigates *Bismarck* and *Marie* put in here. Tell me, what is the news?'

The mail steamer from Mauritius did not call more than once or twice a year.

'The Pope has died,' one of the officers commenced.

'It is too bad,' replied the Creole as his eyes revealed a curiosity. He was surveying coal mounds on deck, the peeling paint, the dented bulkheads and—most appalling of all for a fighting ship—the live stock from the last sinkings.

Emden's officers had become so accustomed to the barnyard aspects that they scarcely noticed, but there they were, in plain view: three surviving pigs rooting around a coal pile 'midships, two sheep tethered to a ventilator, a pigeon cote secured to the centre funnel and several dozen chickens cackling and scratching on the poopdeck.

The visitor pushed back his hat in wonder.

'We've been on a world cruise,' von Müller lied pleasantly, 'and had some trouble in East Africa with the natives . . . decided to come over here to fix up. Also some storms.'

This explanation may or may not have satisfied the Creole. It did amuse von Müller and, later, caused some of the captain's last recorded outbursts of laughter. The *Emden*'s officers did not allow their guest to become more curious. He had a taste for whisky and soda. For the entire three days in harbour his taste was pampered. He seemed fond of the German people.

The days were ones of back-breaking work, transferring coal from the *Markomannia*, shifting ballast from one side of the *Emden* to the other so that the barnacles could be scraped off most of the keel and fresh paint applied, red on the bottom, grey on the sides. The crew went ashore by turn, to walk over the soft, sandy beach and swim in the lagoon which hollowed most of the island like a big saucer. It was safer there than in the surrounding ocean where killer sharks and giant rays ventured up to the *Emden*'s very sides.

With more time, it would have been an extremely pleasant interlude. The war was becoming farther and farther away and many were assuming an air of detachment, daring to dream of a return to the world they knew and loved.

And then, the *Emden* was coaled, scraped and painted. The Creole disembarked in his boat, said good-bye, as the cruiser steamed off to the Bay of Bengal, where war, and death, were real.

By October 20th, *Emden* had sent four more vessels to the bottom, but also sustained a heavy blow herself.

In capturing and sinking the 7,500-ton *Troilus*, a new vessel heavily laden for England with rubber and tin from the Straits Settlement, von Müller was elated. This was a serious loss to the enemy's war factories, measured in terms of millions of pounds as well as military equipment that would never roll.

The eyes of her captain, G. W. Long, moistened, as he watched his command roll under the waves like a stricken creature. He marvelled at how the 'Flying Dutchman' had caught up with him. The *Emden* seemed to be in so many places at once that it was believed she was not one but several cruisers.

But any rejoicing was speedily tempered. The *Emden* could not shepherd the *Markomannia*, *Pontoporos* or *Buresk*. The supply ships often were left by themselves for days at a time while the raider raced after the scent of an enemy merchantman.

On October 15th, the *Markomannia* and *Pontoporos* were off Sumatra. The *Emden* was hard on the chase several hundred miles to the west.

Then the wireless message crackled from the *Markomannia*:

'Under attack. Big British cruiser. Believed *Yarmouth*.'

It was followed by:

'Several hits. Abandoning. . . .'

[92]

That was the last ever heard from the *Markomannia*. The *Emden* was powerless to come to her aid. Von Müller paced solemnly along the bridge, thinking of Captain Faass and the brave crew of the collier. That same evening the English wireless at Colombo confirmed that the *Markomannia* had been sunk by the *Yarmouth* and prisoners taken. The *Pontoporos* had been captured.

Now the *Emden* was left with only the *Buresk* as a collier and supply ship.

Nor did the next three vessels that came along solve a depleted supply problem. The first was a most unusual craft, a new 473-ton dredger, the *Ponrabbel*, en route from the British shipyards to Tasmania. The ungainly contraption, wallowing miserably in the choppy sea, seemed in many respects not worth the trouble to sink. On the other hand, it would perform a vital role in keeping enemy harbours open.

Its captain was not displeased with his capture. He'd been en route for two months, had already been paid for his uncomfortable voyage. He had nothing to lose, except his dredge. And he lost it.

He was given a comfortable cabin to share with his chief engineer, and the two lost no time in opening the case of Scotch they had brought on board.

The *Chilka*, a 5,000-ton passenger steamer, and the somewhat smaller freighter *Benmohr* were captured and sunk in succession about 150 miles south-west of Cochin. An attractive English lady, in her early thirties, detached herself from a curious, apprehensive knot of passengers and walked over to the *Emden*'s boarding officer.

'Well, here we go again,' she observed with a weary smile. 'I was on the *Diplomat*, which you sank back in September, and sent me to Calcutta on the *Kabinga*.'

Then she unfolded her sad story of how she had been trying to hasten home to England when the war overtook her in Hong Kong. After many delays she progressed as far as Singapore, a delay there and then on to Colombo. When she sailed on the Harrison liner *Diplomat* she had every expectation of actually arriving home. That journey interrupted, she was certain that her luck was bound to change . . . then the *Chilka*.

'It's beginning to seem like it's a personal war against me,' she concluded. But, when she arrived on board the *Emden* she walked around distributing chocolates and cigarettes.

Fortunately the *St. Egbert* came along, a good-sized ship, but running in ballast. Von Müller loaded the five hundred odd prisoners from the *Emden* and *Buresk* on to the *St. Egbert*. And that made her captain, W. Barr, very happy. He was given a course to Cochin, and off he went, with his crowded passenger list.

The Admiralty collier *Exford* had the distinction of becoming the *Emden*'s twenty-first prize. Out of Cardiff with a cargo of excellent Welsh coal, it was just the ship von Müller had been looking for. The *Buresk*'s supply of coal was not inexhaustible.

But von Müller was becoming restless, uneasy. The *Emden* must leave the Bay of Bengal again, since enemy cruisers were on the prowl night and day.

'You will have to sail under our orders for a time,' he told Captain H. G. G. Westmore, of the *Exford*. 'We are placing a prize crew aboard.'

Then he instructed his officer who would take command of the *Exford* to proceed to the Cocos Islands and wait for the *Emden* there. This would afford von Müller increased freedom of operation, knowing that the *Emden* could flee from its present area and still have supplies awaiting her.

The night the *Exford* sailed south for a future rendez-vous, the *Emden* was the scene of a happy event. Victoria the cat which had stowed away at Tsingtao gave birth to five kittens. One of the junior officers came off late watch to find them in his hammock swung on the poopdeck.

Beer and rum were broken out so that all hands could toast the newest arrivals. Solemnly, the health of each kitten was drunk as he, or she, was named. They became 'King Lud', 'Foyle', 'Clan Grant', 'Ponrabbel', and 'Chilka'.

On October 26th, von Müller felt impelled to make a decision. No shipping had been observed for five days. Yet, enemy warships were knifing Eastern waters in force. Their very numbers constituted a tribute to his tiny cruiser.

The lights of what was believed to be the *Minotaur* had been sighted through last night's mist. Radio traffic was intercepted with all the volume, and insistence, of back fence gossip from the *Hampshire*, *Yarmouth*, *Ibuki* and somewhat less distinctly from the *Sydney* and *Melbourne* who were sniffing around the west coast of Australia.

There was no question in von Müller's mind: the sixteen or more major warships hunting him down were coming closer and closer. Any one of them was mighty enough to sink *Emden* with the first broadside.

The captain summoned his staff and, bending over the chart table with compass in hand, he explained:

'We will steam on this southerly course, take this easterly leg and then proceed at flank speed into the harbour of Penang at dawn on the 28th. Our mission will be to surprise and destroy enemy warships lying in there . . . the *Montcalm* and *Dupleix*, perhaps.'

The announcement had a sobering effect on his officers. Penang, next to Singapore, was Britain's most important Far Eastern port and naval base . . .

. . . and as the *Emden*'s commander planned his most daring foray yet, the European war continued to gather momentum and amplitude, in acts and in words:

Tsingtao's fall was imminent. The Japanese, led by stubby little General Kamio, were within five miles of the city. A truce had been effected long enough to allow women and children through the lines and into refugee camps. The enemy cruiser *Takachiho*, bombarding the city from the sea, had been sunk by coastal batteries. A British observation plane had plunged into the rice paddies in flames following a spectacular aerial dogfight.

In Berlin, Chancellor von Bethmann-Hollweg expressed the hope that America would preserve her strict neutrality. The retirement of von Moltke as Chief of the General Staff was announced, for reasons of health.

In London, G. K. Chesterton used several columns of type to denounce Prussia as a 'modern Cyclops', while George Bernard Shaw was penning a plea to President Wilson that all warring nations quit ravaged Belgium.

In America, newspaper readers learned from a correspondent's anonymous 'reliable source' in Potsdam that

the war was not the Kaiser's fault but von Moltke's.
And Thomas A. Edison was quoted as saying that
'militarism' was the cause of the war. The *New York
Times* editorialized at length on the exploits of a tiny
cruiser, thrusting about like some modern Robin Hood
half-way around the world:

'. . . the commander of the *Emden* is just now a
most retiring and secretive person.

'. . . she is doing with luck and skill an appointed
task fully legitimatized by the laws of war. The
service she is so efficiently rendering to the Kaiser
is not the highest to which a ship of war can be
assigned, but the worst to be said about it is that
when nations are more civilized than now none of
them will engage in it.

'. . . our own Jones did the same thing the
Emden is doing and even to this day is occasionally
called a pirate by the British. They know, however, that he wasn't one and no more is the commander of the *Emden*.'

CHAPTER 8

MUKA HEAD Light was picked up at midnight, thirty-five miles to the East. Its distinctive yellow flash every twenty seconds was unmistakable.

There were other signs that the raider was fast raising Malaya. A hint of burning sandalwood was already incensing the air. Vegetable growth spread in light, gossamer patches over the flat, shimmering sea as the *Emden* hammered eastward close to its maximum twenty-four knots.

She continued to bear dead-on Muka Head. Then the whoom-whoom of her pistons slowed to a muffled symphony. Von Müller ordered her hove to for several minutes ten miles west of the light which loomed on its rocky sandspit like a winking moon, on-off, on-off.

When satisfied that the surrounding Indian Ocean remained as deserted as it had appeared all evening, he ordered enough headway maintained so the cruiser would not drift seaward.

He squinted, eager to get on with the strike at little Penang Island, only fifteen-and-a-half miles long. It was 300 miles above the Equator, von Müller well knew, and the air with its heat and plant incense drugged sleepers through the night. He would attack at dawn before anyone was in full possession of his faculties.

'Nothing new, Mr. Gropius?' he asked his familiar, nervous question of the navigation officer.

'Nothing new, sir,' was the quick reply.

A lonely commander, with his thoughts his only close companion, von Müller walked the bridge through the new day's early hours. If he was aware by now that he had become legend, he also knew that legends can be quickly dispelled, and forgotten. He preferred to think of himself as just another naval officer, serving his country.

By 3 a.m. it was time to rouse the crew from their deck hammocks or from the sweaty-greasy miasma of their fo'c'sles. The throb of the reciprocating engines was quickening in tempo. Everyone must scrub carefully, as part of the never-ending war on infection, and don fresh clothing.

Clean, and dressed in their newly-laundered linens, the crew once more looked like the young, handsome men they actually were.

Breakfast was hot and ample: oatmeal, sausage and cocoa. Some stomachs might have been tight with anticipation, but the men ate anyhow.

The Southern Cross still burned above like a heavenly manifestation. Yet, being almost on the Equator, the transition into brilliant daylight would be rapid. From the relatively cooling dampness, there would be driving, searing heat—the same sort of shock when a person suddenly opens an oven door.

By 4 a.m. the blacked-out *Emden* was streaking in toward the harbour, her dummy funnel raised.

She swept past Muka Head a few miles to sea. Foaming bow waves rolled out to meet the land, like surf at a bathing beach. No challenge yet. Dark forms materialized ahead, then rushed past, vanished astern—fishing boats.

'Right, left . . .!' The helmsman was hard put to keep up with quickly changing orders. No time for a collision with native dhows or sampans.

Land was almost a physical actuality. The sailors could see lights and smell the cooking fires, the fragrant earth and vegetation as though ashore . . . now racing past Pulo Tikus Light, on a tiny coastal island, then Tokong Point.

Charts showed a police station at Tokong. The policemen were sleeping. Next, following the curving, thickly populated shore . . . the looming profile of a Burmese temple.

Suddenly, at the harbour entrance to Penang, von Müller was startled by a white light which dazzled ahead, then disappeared. A challenge.

'Stand by!' The gunners slammed rounds of ammunition into the breeches of the ten 4.1-inchers, the eight five-pounders, fed clips to the machine-guns. Torpedo tubes swung outward, poised. No tell-tale smoke wisped from the stacks as the *Emden* surged ahead, like some nameless wraith.

The light went off, the sentry satisfied that the stranger was friendly.

The first rays of dawn were flashing into eastern skies, and silhouettes of the mountains which crossed the island like a rugged spine behind the city now were visible. Western Hill, half a mile high and dominating the other peaks, was fringed with pre-dawn clouds, resembling the shaven head of a monk.

[101]

Well ahead, materializing out of the murk was the tall, square Clock Tower. Channel buoys, resembling oriental temples, bobbed and clanged in the *Emden*'s wake.

These were tricky waters, a quagmire of mud and sand flats, all but defying navigation at flank speed at dawn. Between Penang and the mainland the channel was only one-and-a-half miles wide. The ship could almost run aground into the rubber and coconut plantations of Wellesley Province.

Ahead was a forest of ships, at anchor in the roadstead, or warped to the long docks: Sweltenham Pier, Victoria Pier, Church Street Pier, and others. But, no men-of-war? This would be anti-climax, if there were nothing but rusty old coasters in port, like fat ducks in a lagoon, not even worth a four-inch shell.

Then, a dark object loomed mistily, showing three white lights. At first it resembled the stern lamps of three destroyers warped side-by-side in the current.

When six hundred feet abeam, the navigation officer recognized the shape as the Russian cruiser *Jemtchug*: two funnels, about the same size and armament as the *Emden*.

From its darkened, peaceful aspect, there was no indication that anyone, even a look-out, was awake. The order thrilled from bow to stern, then was repeated back . . .

'. . . when on target, FIRE!' Up went *Emden*'s battle flags, like gay, festive bunting.

First a torpedo streaked towards the *Jemtchug*, followed immediately by the deafening salvo of the *Emden*'s broadside guns. They stabbed the murky dawn with red-yellow spits of flame, violating the early serenity.

The shells rained into her forepart, exploding with

small, bright flashes. The torpedo hit aft. There was a
slight upward movement to the Russian as though she
had been caught in a water spout, and she settled back
again with a splash.

Officers rushed from hatchways on to the cruiser's
one low deck. They continued aft and began jumping
over the stern, like so many swimmers at a lake. They
were followed by a horde of sailors streaming up from
the fo'c'sle.

Emden's gunners sprayed them with rapid fire from the
Maxims.

'Wham—wham—wham!'

The *Emden* recoiled like a huge shotgun as another
broadside was hurled at the helpless *Jemtchug*. The
four-inch shells hurtled across the short gap of water like
rattling freight trains as she pirouetted back for another
run.

The forepart of the cruiser looked like a sieve, pocked
with dozens of hotly burning fires. The shells hit, then
fiery rings curled upward, followed by thick, dark
smoke. No one was leaving the wreck now. She was
erupting in volcanoes of sound.

All at once, 'Whistle-rattle-whistle-rattle!' Shells
going over the German's masts and superstructure.

'We are being fired on from three sides!' Gunnery
Officer Gaede exclaimed.

There were geysers as some fell amidst merchantmen
at anchor and at dock. The Russian cruiser, though fast
sinking, and a cauldron of fire and smoke, had managed
to train a couple of her guns into action. But for the
moment, no one could account for the attack from the
other two directions.

Like a slim, shiny porpoise, the second torpedo arrowed away.

The *Emden* heeled far over as she made a sharp, high-speed turn to port, preparing to boil back for still a third torpedo, also to elude the desultory shower of projectiles overhead.

'Crash-b-lam!'

The early morning now shook with one thunderous explosion, which reverberated to the mountains, then echoed back. A thick cloud of black smoke, mixed with sparks and grey streaks of steam and spray from the harbour water towered hundreds of feet into the blue sky. It hid everything from view as *Emden* wheeled again, its crew clutching handholds to keep from being thrown on to the deck. For a moment guns were silent, leaving only the fast 'whoom-whoom-whoom' of straining pistons, up-down, up-down. . . .

As the *Emden* raced towards the scene, the smoke lifted. The cruiser was gone.

Her masthead poked above the choppy waters. Sampans and other native craft were putting out from shore to pick up survivors.

It was light enough to see the city clearly, the serrated roof rows of its white houses, green palms, the grey, dirty piers. Inhabitants were awakened. The excited sing-song of the Chinese, Tamils and Malays of this sweltering Straits settlement babbled as they rushed into the narrow, smelling streets.

The source of the other shooting was revealed—two French gunboats at anchor among the merchantmen, which identification charts indicated were the *D'Iberville* and *Pistolet*. Obviously, they did not have steam up and were unable to pursue. They were short, stubby, two-stackers.

Churning the Penang channel, the *Emden* swung in after them when the masthead look-out, in his vantage point above the searchlights, reported a hostile destroyer steaming in from sea.

Von Müller made an 180-degree turn, narrowly missing a lumbering sampan, and sped out to meet her.

There was no longer reason for secrecy. The black smoke poured from *Emden*'s funnels and fell on to her wake. As armour plate, sometimes a foot or more thick, is the protection of a battleship, fleetness was the *Emden*'s almost sole defence.

In a few minutes, the other ship could be distinguished bearing in. She had a high pointed fo'c'sle, with a low, wide funnel, typical of a new class of fast English destroyers.

At long range, 12,000 feet, the first shot. It lobbed over her and kicked a column of water up astern. She turned hard to starboard.

'It's only a British government steamer . . . !' Gropius exclaimed.

It was perhaps the cable ship plying monotonously to Butterworth across this narrow neck of the Malacca Straits. The morning light in the tropics could play tricks.

As the *Emden* turned to press the attack once more on the *D'Iberville* and *Pistolet*, the terrified steamer abruptly slowed, stopped altogether, as though her skipper had beached her to keep from being sunk.

Ahead, puffs of white came from the funnels of the anchored merchantmen. They were blowing whistles nervously.

The mountains behind the city had become impressive. The early mist was moving higher to the summits as the day's warmth mounted. Swarming over the stark, rough hillsides, the coolies were already tilling their rocky gardens.

The sky was becoming tinted with rainbow hues, from an increasingly deep scarlet to delicate pink. But daylight presaged danger for a lone cruiser. There could be heavier warships farther down, which the *Emden* could defeat only by a surprise attack.

Again the look-out called:

'*Kriegsschiffe!*'

It looked at first like a warship approaching the straits, but this time it was identified as a good-sized merchantman.

A cutter was lowered, with an officer in command and half a dozen seamen, all armed with pistols, and steamed across the harbour to meet her.

The merchantman hove to and was waiting. The British flag hung limply at the stern, the name in dirty gold: *Glen Turret*.

'We'll only have time to open her sea valves,' the officer rumbled, with a look at the rapidly brightening skies.

The boarders were just coming alongside the rope ladder uncoiled down the *Glen Turret*'s rust-caked port side when sirens wailed from the *Emden*:

'. . . whoo-p, whoo-p . . . !'

Recall! Even as the ragged lot of sailors who peered over the towering decks of the freighter gaped in relief, the tiller was put hard over and the cutter steamed back to the cruiser as fast as the one-cycle engine would drive it.

For the third time, the *Emden* was hurrying out to meet an unidentified inbound vessel. The party in the cutter was picked up, even as the cruiser swayed with gathering speed, like a racehorse.

The refraction of the light rays again was making identification difficult. First it would seem to be a large, black ship, with funnels fore and aft. Then the dimensions would shrink, half the funnels disappear and she would resemble a grey merchantman with black funnel bands.

In a couple of minutes she proved to be small, did have two black funnels, far apart, and was low to the water with little or no superstructure. She was a French torpedo boat destroyer, probably the *Mousquet*.

When still 18,000 feet off, she ran up the Tricolour. She altered course, kicking up spray like a speed-boat, and attempted to come on at right angles, as though manœuvring to launch a torpedo.

Emden turned to port, now at 11,000 feet range, and let go a broadside at the *Mousquet*.

She heeled and started to run. Gunners were ejecting shells and reloading like lightning-fast, precision machines. The second salvo . . . then, a third . . .

. . . five shells from the last salvo lodged aft in the torpedo boat, and there was a heavy detonation. A boiling cloud of black coal dust and steam enveloped her stern and the concussion was felt on the *Emden*. The magazine had gone up, as it had on the *Jemtchug*.

Even so, the little vessel launched two torpedoes. *Emden* wheeled, and they bubbled past to starboard. Her shells were clattering through the German's rigging.

Another broadside from the *Emden* . . . the enemy's

guns were silenced, her mast, her two funnels, her ventilators, bridge, almost her entire superstructure were shot away. She went lower and lower beneath the smoke, steam and fire spewing heavenward.

In a few more minutes the *Mousquet* disappeared.

Von Müller ordered speed slowed one-quarter, and a medical launch put over the side. The surgeons, their assistants and a complete supply of medical equipment including even splints and emergency operating kits, were soon speeding to the scene. A ship had gone down, leaving only its pitiful, thrashing human flotsam in the disturbed waters.

The wheeze from the cutter's steam engine and the background heavier throb of the *Emden* as she described a wide circle alone disturbed the sudden peacefulness of the Malacca Straits. Mountains to the east were picking up the first rays of the sun. Buildings at the water's edge were etched in the morning's brilliance.

The cutter pushed through the debris to the French sailors. Oil-soaked and coughing, they clutched spars, life preservers, wood gratings, any bit of wreckage which floated.

They were frightened. Some shrieked and flailed the waters as they fought off rescue attempts.

One was pulled, still struggling, over the gunwales. His eyes were wide with terror. A few wore their jaunty French naval caps, and this appeared incongruous.

Soon they had given up resisting rescue and were hauled aboard the cutter. The doctor worked rapidly, winding on the dressings . . . every so often the glint from his scalpel . . . the whimperings of pain . . . fractured arms and legs put in splints . . . amputations.

Finally, thirty-three Frenchmen were counted. A young officer, who shivered under two blankets wrapped around him, began talking in broken German. He admitted that the *Mousquet* had been the sentry vessel that blinked at dawn. She mistook the *Emden* for the *Yarmouth*.

Her gallant captain had both legs shot away in the second salvo. He had ordered his quartermaster to tie him to the binnacle, so he could direct the fight even as his ship disintegrated beneath him. He was seen there, alive, as the *Mousquet* went under.

'. . . some of us swam away because we believed newspaper reports that Germans massacred prisoners. We did not want to be butchered,' he concluded.

The *Emden*'s radio operator had in the meanwhile intercepted a message from Penang wireless:

'German cruiser *Emden* just entered harbour, sinking Russian cruiser and French destroyer *Mousquet*.'

The beached government steamer remained fast on her sandbar, though belching smoke in a change-of-heart attempt to free herself. The *Glen Turret* had vanished inside the sheepfold of anchored merchantmen. The *D'Iberville* and *Pistolet* were in their same positions.

The sun was over the mountains now and bathing rugged Penang Island in tropical brilliance. It was time to move. The units of the British, Australian, Japanese and Russian fleets could not be far over the horizon, von Müller suspected.

'Full speed ahead!'

The order was welcome. The *Emden*'s bow lifted perceptibly as she knifed the water into port and star-board waves. The gunners were swabbing the hot breeches of their weapons, and greasing the firing mechanisms. Soap, buckets, brushes and mops were appearing on the decks.

Penang's clock tower shrank astern, the government buildings and piers faded into a vague blur beneath the ship masts. The shoreline of equatorial vegetation, bright green palms and duller, stubbier banana trees swept past like a long, moving smudge.

'Astern . . . !' the alarm rang out.

There was the *Pistolet*, steam up at last and bouncing in pursuit under an umbrella of spray.

'Let us meet her in the open sea,' von Müller said.

Course was continued westward, past Tokong Point, Pulo Tikus, towering, impressive Muka Head Light, 748 feet high on its rocky bluff . . . and the empty reaches of the sparkling Indian Ocean.

The *Pistolet* trailed doggedly until she was swallowed by a rain squall off Muka Head. Von Müller was no longer interested in taking time to make contact with the game little Frenchman.

'Full speed ahead!' was the standing order to the engine-room, as the helmsman steered a westward course.

Penang seemed destined already to be immortalized in German history along with such Franco-Prussian symbols of victory as Sedan and Metz, or Tannenberg already in this war. On the other hand, von Müller knew that any elation must be tempered by reality. The sands could not trickle downwards in the raider's hour-glass indefinitely.

He kept to his bridge. 'Nothing new, Mr. Gropius?'

'MY raid on the Cocos group,' von Müller logged, 'was determined by the following considerations:

'Apart from the material damage the enemy would have suffered by the destruction of the cable and wireless stations and the temporary interruption of telegraphic communications between Australia on the one hand and England and other countries on the other, I hoped also to effect (1) a general unrest among shipping to and from Australia by creating the impression that the *Emden* would proceed to harry the steamer traffic south and west of Australia and (2) a withdrawal from the Indian Ocean of at least some of the English cruisers which were taking part in the hunting down of the *Emden*. My intention was, after carrying out the raid on the Cocos group, to make for Socotra and cruise in the Gulf of Aden, and then on the steamer-route between Aden and Bombay.'

He planned even as the memory of Penang remained fresh, in a peculiar emotional balance of grief and triumph. The *Jemtchug* and the *Mousquet* were at the bottom of the Malacca Straits, enemy shipping further paralyzed. Yesterday, on the other hand, he had buried two French sailors at sea. They had succumbed to their wounds.

Wrapped in sailcloth, and covered with the Tricolour,

the bodies rested on the starboard boom as von Müller spoke in French and in German. He paid tribute to the sailors as having died a hero's death for their country, and then recited:

'The Lord is my shepherd, therefore can I lack nothing. He shall feed me in a green pasture, and lead me forth beside the waters of comfort . . .'

As he concluded the burial service, he read:

'. . . the Lord gave and the Lord hath taken away, blessed be the name of the Lord.'

The solemn words had hardly grown silent when three salvoes were fired into the air, and the bodies were committed to the sea.

It was depressing for everyone. Von Müller retired to his cabin for a short time before returning to the bridge, while the chant of the crew themselves had recently composed assumed a deeper, sadder meaning:

> *Schiff ohne Hafen, Schiff ohne Ruh,*
> *Fliegende, fliegende* Emden *du.*
> *Kannst ja nicht sterben, es jagt daher*
> *Ewig dein Schatten über das Meer . . . !*

They sang with a weariness, this threnody of a ship without a harbour, men without a home, without rest, or even but the slimmest hope of personal salvation.

On November 1st, the remaining French prisoners of war had been transferred to the S.S. *Newburn*, loaded with salt, which appeared on the horizon one morning. Among them was the only surviving French officer. His leg had been amputated by the *Emden*'s doctor.

The German crew lined the decks of the *Emden* and saluted as the *Newburn* sailed off to Khota Raja, Sumatra, where a hospital was situated.

On November 2nd, news was received of a naval victory the day before. Admiral von Spee, whom the *Emden* had left three eventful months ago at Pagan Island, had sunk the British armoured cruisers *Good Hope* and *Monmouth* in a battle off Coronel, Chile. Led by the mighty *Gneisenau* and *Scharnhorst*, von Spee's squadron had scored a smashing defeat over that of Admiral Sir Christopher Cradock. How many other Royal Navy ships had been damaged the wireless did not advise.

One broadcast, from Colombo, reported the 'beautiful spectacle' of the British squadron steaming away from the snow-capped Andes towering above the Chilean coast. The afternoon sun shone bright as a heavy wind whipped spindrift back across the foredecks. Von Spee found it quite a spectacle himself.

On November 3rd the *Emden* put in at Simalur, this time to recoal from the *Buresk*. The fuel transfer had been in progress barely an hour when a small launch put out from the shore, and came alongside.

'We are sorry not to have been ready with appropriate honours,' the *Emden*'s officer of the deck apologized. 'You see, we mistook you for a fishing vessel.'

He was not intentionally trying to rib the Dutch officer. The dirty launch suggested a fishing smack. But the Dutchman did not laugh.

'It may interest you to know,' he said with an air of doom, 'that Portugal has just declared war on Germany.'

Von Müller chuckled audibly in reply, since Portugal

did not impress him as being formidable. However, he hastened to assure the officer that *Emden* was outside the three-mile territorial limits, then offered him a drink of whisky.

The cruiser finished its coaling, and the Dutchman his drink.

Emden cruised for a short time in the Sunda Straits. There von Müller, as a student of naval history, was aware that the famous Confederate raider *Alabama* had captured and burned three prizes half a century before. Commander Raphael Semmes, 'Old Beeswax', was in many respects, including a disarming gentleness, ancestor to von Müller himself.

The German cruiser's luck in the Straits was not as fruitful. She encountered no enemy shipping. Soon she was sailing past the famous volcano Krakatau whose massive eruption in 1883 killed more than 36,000 people and sent a cloud of smoke and ash literally around the world.

At this same time, von Müller's friend, Captain Erich Köhler, and three-quarters of his crew perished when the *Karlsruhe* blew up mysteriously off the Barbados. Neither von Müller nor the British Navy were to learn of the loss for months.

Before von Müller quit the Sunda area he conducted a brief ceremony. He promoted Torpedo Machinist's Mate Pyttlik to Torpedo Machinist for his excellent service at Penang. At the same time, von Müller emphasized that the demands of this detached operation made it impossible to promote and otherwise honour all others of his crew who might also have distinguished themselves.

The officers celebrated with a glass of champagne in

von Müller's cabin. Then he was back on the bridge, making sure that his navigating officer had not neglected to inform him of anything.

'Nothing new, Mr. Gropius?'

And so, finally, the Captain of the *Emden* decided on his foray, away from his general raiding area, against the Cocos Islands. In addition to the reasons he chronicled, the assault would serve the increasingly necessary purpose: keep in action, keep going, never stop, always a new goal. The inertia of lull moments could easily upset forever the tenuous balance so critical to a raider known as morale.

The *Emden* ploughed towards the infinitesimal cluster of atolls, 600 miles south-west of Java. None was more than twenty feet above sea level at the highest elevation. The Keelings, or Cocos, were ruled under a 999-year patent by the J. Clunies Ross family, and thought of by their inhabitants as a 'paradise on earth', by Charles Darwin as 'typical lagoon atolls.'

Otherwise, these specks of coral, at the mercy of wind and sea, useful only in the communication nerves of Empire, were unknown to the world.

The *Emden*'s accomplishments now totalled more than 100,000 tons of enemy shipping sunk, valued, with their cargoes, at perhaps as high as three hundred and sixty thousand pounds. This included the hapless Japanese freighter, the *Kamagasaki Maru*, which was dispatched as the Emden ploughed south. Her chattering crew was bustled into lifeboats to await the *Buresk*.

Von Müller was proud of one thing: he had caused the loss of life of not one civilian non-combatant.

The German commander was not blundering rashly

into the Cocos mission. He knew he could monitor wireless messages to and from the Eastern Extension Telegraph Company on Direction Island for a clue as to warships in the vicinity.

As the first week of November wore on, it became evident that there was a break in the Cocos' protection. And that break was Australia's first convoy of troops for Europe, preparing to sail from Perth. The *Sydney* and *Melbourne*, of the Royal Australian Navy, and possibly the *Minotaur*, *Hampshire*, *Ibuki* and all the rest which had been pursuing *Emden* would be escorting the important convoy.

On the other hand, the thought of lunging at this mighty assemblage apparently never occurred to von Müller, who could temper boldness with discretion. Suicidal tendencies were actually not present in his otherwise complex character.

Sad news arrived on November 6th: the wireless reported the fall of Tsingtao. Victorious British and Japanese troops were in the city. Prisoner camps were being established.

It was the end of German colonial dreams in China. It was also the end of *Emden*'s home port, theoretical as it had been for many weeks. Where now could the cruiser's complement turn for rest?

Not a man dared even hint this question.

Von Müller's report continued:

'On November 7th, about 8 p.m., the *Emden* arrived at its appointed rendezvous with the *Exford* . . . 30 miles north of the North Keeling Island. The *Exford* . . . was then to proceed to a rendezvous about 900 miles away in the direction of Socotra, await the *Emden* there as long as her provisions lasted, and then, if we did not turn up, run for a neutral harbour.'

Men-of-war birds, themselves associated with the Keelings, screeched overhead in the darkness, as the two vessels floated side by side. The *Exford* was as filthy as the *Emden* herself . . . the one-time 'Swan of the East' cruiser was a sight: decks dusty from coal heaps, rusty bulkheads, scars and dents, a pigeon cote beside the funnel, one surviving pig tethered to a stanchion, the distinctive acrid, seaweedy reek that a ship assumes after it has been cruising far too long. To veteran salts it smelled like the sunken trawlers which were towed into Wilhelmshaven after being raised off the Frisians.

. . . at that very time, as the cruiser coaled, and thousands of miles across the Pacific, the *Geier*, which had bid adieu to the *Emden* in August, steamed into Honolulu and allowed herself to be interned.

Just before dawn, as the gulls greeted the new day with their raucous matins, the *Exford* pushed off. Lauterbach was in command. There was a growing hum, a thump-thump and a whoom quickly blending into one continuous, muffled roar as the pistons returned to life. They shook the cruiser, as a big man would shake his bed as he awakes and stretches.

The *Exford* swept astern as the sky reddened in the east.

But other things, beside the coaling of a German warship, had been going on in the reaches of the Indian Ocean. Every hour the Cocos wireless station was sending out a message in three-figure cypher preceded by the word 'urgent'. No answer followed at first and it seemed to von Müller that this was a secret communication to passing traders.

[117]

Finally, after the *Exford* had vanished over the western horizon, an English warship using the signal letters 'NC' acknowledged the 'urgent' message flashing through the skies from the Cocos.

Emden kept close monitor through the morning. The interchange between warship and shore station grew heavier. What was the enemy craft? The letters indicated the light cruiser *Newcastle*, but from operations as plotted by von Müller's own intelligence, it might have been the heavy cruiser *Minotaur*.

Before noon, the traffic tapered off, and the ship's replies grew increasingly faint. When it ceased altogether by early afternoon, the navigation officer estimated the warship to be about 200 miles away, to the north-east. He further reasoned that it was proceeding from Sunda Strait, between Java and Sumatra to the Cape Colony. There a rebellion under de Wet had flared into a certain violence.

Since no more wireless messages were intercepted from any warship during the afternoon, it was a reasonable conclusion that the enemy was no longer in the vicinity.

'I had intended to attack the Cocos group on the 8th,' von Müller stated, 'but postponed the operation for a day because of the unusual hourly messages picked up during the night of 7th–8th November and because I had not yet met the *Exford*. When on the morning of the 8th I picked up the warship's conversation with the shore station, I debated whether I should not delay for another day. I gave up this idea, however, as I reckoned that next morning the English warship would be quite far enough away; further I had to consider the state of my coal-supply, since my nearest safe coaling-station on the way to Socotra was at Addu Atoll in the southern Maldives, about 1,500 miles off.

'I had to reckon with the presence—not very probable, but still possible—of an enemy cruiser stationed in the group to protect the cable and wireless stations; as I did not wish to expose my collier to the risk of destruction, or even of damage by shellfire, I ordered the *Buresk* to wait 30 miles north of the South Keeling group, and not to rejoin me unless she received wireless orders to do so.

'If the situation proved favourable, I intended to use the opportunity for coaling.'

The crew was treated to a sumptuous Sunday dinner: the last chickens which had been cackling in the crates, complete with yams and preserves from Edinburgh . . . memories of the *Clan Grant*.

At less than one-third speed, the *Emden* cruised in erratic circles off the northern approaches to the Cocos group that still, sultry Sunday night. No one could sleep as a now familiar routine was repeated . . . scrub, dress in fresh clothing, jettison papers, cartons, anything easily inflammable, meticulous preparations in the surgery, ready boxes opened, fuses set on assorted pre-determined ranges.

While the men snatched rest in off-duty hours, they smoked cigarettes, black cigars, or shuffled greasy packs of cards. From one fo'c'sle came the mandolin strains of the popular 'Rose of Stamboul', monotonously, until mounting complaints from another fo'c'sle persuaded the musician to change his tune.

He did, to 'Tipperary'. Everyone thought that was funny. It served to break the tension momentarily. Some voices joined in a jeering chorus.

A few men read their Bibles or Missals, or wrote letters. But it was weeks since any mail had been posted. Even von Müller had not written to his mother or sister Elfreda, in Blankenburg, for ten days or more. His middle desk drawer already contained several notes to them. Perhaps at the next neutral port . . . though neutrals were becoming fewer and fewer in this mountingly wild war.

The engines throbbed, muffled, the water lapped past the sides, punctuating in its small, sensitive way the passage of time. Once again, land was nearing, and tropical pungence scented the air.

At 5.30 a.m., as the sun rose, *Emden* picked up tiny Horsborough Island. It poked shyly out of the tropical waters like the glistening head of an otherwise bald man with a few remaining hairs on the very top.

The sky was red to the east, over Direction Island, as the water turned purplish blue. The men-o'-war birds glided back overhead, noisy, guttural welcomers. No enemy vessel was to be seen.

A little after 6 a.m., the *Emden*, her fourth funnel in place, dropped anchor in Port Refuge. The engines were stopped, fires half-banked to save coal. But there was sufficient steam in the boilers to enable her to get under way at a moment's notice.

As soon as the anchor was dropped, the landing party boarded boats. The ever able first officer von Muecke and two junior lieutenants, Gyssling and Schmidt, took command of approximately fifty men, armed with machine guns, rifles, sidearms, axes, belt-knives, grappling hooks, and explosives for demolition.

On the other hand they presented contrasts since

they were clean-shaven, immaculate in tropical helmets and high ankle boots, as though ready to march in parade. Too, they were perhaps as handsome a raiding party as ever struck out for an enemy island . . . bearing no resemblance, in appearance or purpose, to the piratical tradition of Kidd, Blackbeard, or Morgan.

They swept towards the island, having no idea what reception awaited.

'. . . von Muecke had my orders to destroy the cable and wireless stations and if possible to cut the cables: first the Australian, next the South African, then that to the Dutch Indies,' von Müller wrote. 'All code books and records of messages were to be brought aboard. A recall signal was agreed on. Verbally I told Lieutenant-Commander von Muecke that, if the island was in a state of defence and garrisoned, I would give up the plan of landing and confine myself to bombarding the wireless and telegraphic stations, as a loss of personnel in this enterprise was to be avoided at all costs—this in view of the raiding campaign later. The *Emden*'s wireless had received orders to drown at once any wireless signals from the island.

'As conditions in Port Refuge were favourable for coaling, and no enemy warship seemed to be in the immediate vicinity, I had a wireless message sent to the *Buresk* as soon as the boats neared the landing-stage, ordering her to join the *Emden* forthwith. The *Buresk* did not answer, as her transmitter was out of order. For this eventuality the arrangement had been made that the wireless signal to rejoin should be repeated three times . . . the island station then asked:

' "What code? What ship is that?" '

'We naturally did not answer.

'Soon afterwards the island station began to talk, and in spite of our interruptions, the message, "Strange ship off entrance!" got through.

'A little while later a warship or auxiliary cruiser whose signal letters had not been heard previously in the war was heard to call up the island, but received no answer . . .

'By resistance-measurements the distance of the enemy ship was estimated at 200 to 250 miles. I now abandoned my intention of coaling and cancelled the arrangements made for it . . .'

Several times another message crackled through the air,

'S O S Cocos . . . ! S O S Cocos . . . !'

Von Müller lit a fresh cigarette as he nervously paced the bridge and wished the landing party would hurry up and blast the wireless transmitter off the air.

And, meanwhile, von Muecke and his raiders sat silently in the three launches and watched the *Emden* shrinking astern. Direction Island loomed ever closer. Its luxuriant palm trees were taking shape, a line of a dozen, low, white buildings, guarded by the high radio mast.

It was just another copra island, punctuating the world's seas. It was except for one thing—it harboured a wireless and cable station.

The boats pushed past an old schooner lying at anchor. The name *Ayesha* showed on the stern's half-rotted planking.

Von Muecke continued on toward a pier, as his men clutched their guns more tightly.

CHAPTER 10

THE previous night, Darcy Farrant, the able,
thorough superintendent of the Eastern Extension
Telegraph Company, had slept fitfully. He was
not sure whether it was the tinned beef he had eaten for
supper, or—what?

The very air was charged with uneasy apprehension.
Several times he had got out of bed, and walked into
the hot transmitter rooms to check with the sweaty
operators on watch, then padded down to the beach to
peer into the dark, star-studded night. The sea had a
beguiling complacency as it lap-lapped, lap-lapped.

He wrote:*

'At 5.50 a.m. on the 9th I was informed that a warship
with four funnels was steaming for the entrance between
Horsborough and Direction Islands. Quickly investi-
gating, and finding that the fourth funnel was palpably
canvas, I found Mr. C. H. K. La Nauze and instructed
him to proceed immediately to the wireless hut, and to
put out a general call that there was a strange warship in
our vicinity, asking for assistance, and signing our naval
code. At the same time I proceeded to the office and
sent services, as previously instructed, to London,
Adelaide, Perth and Singapore.

'The *Emden* (for such she turned out to be) came in at

* *Official History of Australia in the War of 1914–18*, by Arthur W. Jones,
Angus and Robertson, Ltd., Sydney.

[123]

a great speed nearly as far as our outer buoy, where she wheeled and disclosed an armoured launch and two heavily manned boats under her counter. They were immediately slipped and speeded straight for the jetty. Through a glass we managed to distinguish four machine-guns, two in the launch and one in the bow of each boat. The information was conveyed to the aforementioned stations, and I personally told Singapore that it was the *Emden*.

'So quick had been their movements, evidently with the hope of rushing our wireless, that the slip of the last-mentioned services was passing through the 'Autos' when they entered the office.

'In the meantime, Mr. La Nauze was putting out the call. I returned to the wireless hut, where he informed me that the *Emden* and her collier the *Buresk* were endeavouring to interrupt him. I instructed him to continue the call, as the fact of forcing the two ships to use their strong Telefunken notes could only be regarded as a matter for suspicion if picked up by a warship.

'I stood at the corner of the hut to assume responsibility for the use of the wireless, until an officer and some half-dozen blue-jackets ordered us to desist and leave. Armed guards ran to all buildings, and the office was taken possession of in force and the staff ordered out.

'Lieutenant von Muecke, in charge of the landing party, was exceedingly agreeable. He informed me that he had landed three officers and forty men, and his instructions were to destroy the cable and wireless station. Further than this, he said, they would not go, and all private property would be respected. He instructed me to collect the staff and take them to a place of safety, as he was blowing up the wireless mast.'

In Perth, a young Royal Australian Navy signalman was electrified by the flash that came over his keyboard from the lonely Cocos station.

'Very urgent. Do not reply. Warship here, three funnels. Landing men at 7 a.m.'

Some fifty miles north of Farrant's station, the Australian convoy's escort was equally electrified. The *Sydney, Melbourne, Minotaur, Ibuki* and lesser cruisers and destroyers, determined that not one sideplate of their precious charges would be scratched, had all heard the plea for help, direct from the busy La Nauze's own key, and relayed in code from Perth, Adelaide and even Singapore. In those bases, His Majesty's Naval officers were almost intoxicated with excitement at the prospect of their common nemesis, *Emden*, at last cornered.

The *Sydney* ordered steam up to the bursting point. She pointed her long, low bow to the south and left the convoy erupting thick, billowing clouds of black smoke. She was, and looked, a ship possessed in her eagerness to close on a lesser prey.

For her Captain, John C. T. Glossop, this appeared the windfall of his lifetime of forty-three years. He somehow had no doubts that his command would be equal to their unexpected destiny.

The escorting screen he had left behaved in a grimly humorous manner, jealous of *Sydney's* prerogative. *Melbourne*, rearranging the stations to fill in the gap left by *Sydney*, signalled the *Ibuki*. Much to the former's surprise, the *Ibuki* already had battle-flags hoisted, her decks cleared for action, and was boiling away at top speed to join the *Sydney*.

With blunt persuasion, the Japanese warship, disappointed, slunk back to her position on the south-western flank . . . and the convoy continued ahead to Suez and the Mediterranean where fresh soldiers would be disembarked in France.

Inside the largest building on Direction Island, von Muecke had located Farrant, whom he thought of as a 'portly Englishman', waiting calmly in his shirt-sleeves. He handed over a bunch of keys to von Muecke.

The Germans went about their task systematically, swinging axes at instruments, dynamos, batteries, ink bottles, anything that could conceivably be needed for wireless or cable transmission. Even rolls of message tape were torn, unrolled across the floors and scuffed over.

Some inconsequential machinery went the way of the wireless and telegraphic equipment, which had succumbed amidst showers of sparks. A seismometer, useful only in detecting and measuring earthquakes, was one innocent victim to the flaying axes.

Von Muecke was impressed by Farrant's cordiality and interpreted the latter's glances at a tennis racquet propped against a corner of his office as a desire for a match. The *Emden*'s first officer noticed how well maintained the little settlement was; the paths were kept smooth with powdered coral, gardens and vegetation were well tended. There also appeared to be every facility for a person's comfort: mess halls, billiard room, tennis court, stores, in addition to the machinery sheds and a hut for coolie servants, across the island. There was everything in fact, but women and money. Both against the rules, were considered too fertile a source of provocation and discord.

Von Muecke had an unexpected distraction. Superintendent Farrant informed him, amidst congratulations, that a Reuter dispatch had announced the Iron Cross had been conferred on the *Emden's* first officer.

As von Muecke recorded:

'We now set to work to tear down the wireless tower. The men in charge of the torpedoes quickly set them in place. The stays that supported the tower were demolished first, and then the tower itself was brought down and chopped into kindling wood.'

'. . . To locate and cut the submarine cables was the most difficult part of our task. A chart, showing the direction in which the cables extended, was not to be found in the station, but close to the shore we discovered a number of signboards, bearing the inscription, CABLES. This, therefore, must be the place where we must search for the ends of the cable strands.'

'Back and forth the steam launch carried us over the cables that were plainly to be seen in the clear water as we tried to grasp them with a couple of drags and heavy dredging hooks, which we drew along the bottom. It was no light task, for the cables were very heavy and the only power at our command was a very limited amount of human strength. For a while it seemed impossible to draw the cables to the surface; in the end, after we had succeeded in raising the bight of the cable a little, my men had to get into the water, dive and tie tackle to it, by the aid of which we continued our labour.'

'With great difficulty we at length succeeded in getting

[127]

the cable strands into the boat. I did not want to use any of the dynamite charges for the work of destruction, as the *Emden* might have need of them for the sinking of more steamers. So we set to work upon the stout cables with crowbars, axes, driving chisels, and other like implements. After long and weary labour, we succeeded in cutting through two of them, and we then dragged the ends out to sea, and dropped them there. The third cable was not to be found in spite of our diligent search for it.

'A small house of corrugated iron, in which were stored quantities of reserve apparatus and all sorts of duplicate parts, was blown up and set on fire with a couple of explosive cartridges. All newspapers, books, Morse tapes, and the like, we took away with us.'

Farrant watched, hidden satisfaction alleviating his natural dismay. The top part of the wireless mast was only partly destroyed, and he was sure his men could hoist it up again.

'The only question I was asked,' he was to note, 'was the whereabouts of the cable ends; the answer "in the sea" appeared to satisfy them, as I was not pressed. Whilst all the damage was being done ashore, the launch was searching the foreshore for our cables, and I noted with delight that she first raised a small type (probably B), which would be our half-naut. of spare laid out in the lagoon. The greater part of her time was taken up in coiling this cable inboard, and it did not appear to strike them that there was a considerable slack for a laid cable.

'Later they raised Perth, which they experienced very

View of the damage done to the *Emden*'s deck from the fore-castle

mden, taken from the port bow

The starboard waist of the *Emden*, looking aft

The *Emden* wreck, tak
from the starboard bea

great difficulty in cutting . . . the cut was made about 300 yards from the jetty.

'At about 8.45 a.m. the *Emden* steamed in again, and made frantic endeavours to recall her boats, using both her flags and sirens. The launch appeared to be unwilling to give up her cable and some delay was experienced in getting her in and the men aboard.'

That Farrant was not as calm as he appeared was evident by the fact that the *Emden* had not weighed anchor yet. But von Muecke knew she soon would, as he read her successively more urgent signals: the blinker to 'hurry work!' the siren to return with utmost dispatch, and finally her anchor flag flying at half mast, which announced the 'hook' was being hauled aboard.

'All my effort was bent on getting back to the ship as speedily as possible,' von Muecke reported. 'With all steam on we raced toward the *Emden* taking the shortest course between the reefs.

'Meanwhile the *Emden* had turned seaward and was running at high speed out of the harbour. My first thought was that she was going to meet our tender, the *Buresk*, that had been ordered here with coal and which I supposed was going to pilot us through the reefs. In this belief I continued to follow *Emden* as fast as I could but was surprised to find her going at a speed of from sixteen to seventeen miles. Our launch, with the heavily laden cutters in tow, could make barely four miles an hour.

'Suddenly we saw the battle flags on the *Emden* run up, and then a broadside burst from her starboard. Even yet the reason for all this was hidden from me and

I

I believed the *Emden* to be in pursuit of a steamer that had come in view.

'But now a salvo of five heavy shells struck the water just aft of the *Emden*; five tall waterspouts marked the places where they fell into the sea. There was no longer any room for doubt; we knew that a battle was on in earnest.

'The *Emden*'s opponent we could not see, for the island, with its tall palms, was between us. The *Emden* in the meantime had increased her distance from us to several thousand metres, and was adding to her speed with every moment.

'All hope of overtaking her had therefore to be abandoned and I turned back.'

It was at about this time that Farrant and La Nauze were interrupted at breakfast and hurried out to see what was going on. There had never been a scene like it in the Cocos group . . . or anywhere else in the Indian Ocean.

And 50 miles to the north the *Ibuki* was again pleading excitedly for permission to leave the convoy, as her short, smiling crewmen adjusted their eye-glasses and chattered in Japanese, beside their guns.

THE crew waited, almost not daring to breathe, for the first salvo. It was a 'ranging' salvo, yet lives, even a measure of the future of Germany depended on it.

The *Emden* plunged ahead on its north-westerly course over the blue waters, their flatness disturbed only by a ground swell. The sun beat so hotly that the crew wished they could remove the shirts worn as protection against powder burns and infection.

A small cloud of birds, which had been wheeling lazily over the cruiser, flapped towards the tiny, coral crescent of North Keeling Island.

One, two, three, four, five . . . the seconds ticked away. A slight alteration of course to the north . . . the surge of steel deck pressing harder under foot, as the cruiser heaved into the turn.

'*Zu links . . .* !' the look-out cried. The salvo had fallen to the left, well on the other side of the *Sydney*. The water plumed in neat, white geysers, as the shells detonated throatily.

This first salvo actually had been only a hundred yards short, remarkable accuracy for a 'ranging' shot. Captain Glossop, of the *Sydney*, not yet prepared to open fire, had been taken by surprise at the sudden assumption of the offensive.

It was followed up, in seconds. Fast passing of new

ranges, new deflections, on target . . . blam! . . .
decks heaving in a second armageddon of sound, smoke
and flashing light, stunning recoil, the hot, acrid blast in
the face. The second salvo clattered across open water
with the erratic metallic sound of a freight train banging
in the stillness of night . . . short . . . two more
salvoes, short . . . seconds turning into minutes.

It was 9.30.

On shore, at the Cable Station, Farrant was now standing on his office roof and observing the battle, as he might
a cricket match. He wrote:

'The *Emden* worked her guns splendidly, and seemed
to be firing continually. Her shells were plainly visible,
cutting through the black smoke of the *Sydney*, and she
appeared to be making good shooting. The *Sydney*, on
the other hand, having to pick up her range by gunfire,
was at first somewhat handicapped, her shells landing
over or short of the other cruiser and apparently somewhat astern.

'They had, no doubt, underestimated her speed, as she
was travelling at a fast rate.'

While on the *Sydney* blood had been drawn. Signalman Seabrooke recalled why it was that his cruiser was
having to 'pick up her range by gunfire'. He described
the *Emden*'s first hit:

'. . . and a right smart hit it was, too, though its
results were by no means so bad as they might have been.
I had the finest kind of a chance to see everything that
that first shell did to us. It began by cutting off a pair of
signal-halyards on the engaged side, then tore a leg off
the range-taker, then sheared off the stand supporting
the range-finder itself, then through the hammocks

[132]

lining the inside of the upper bridge and finally down through the canvas screen of the signal bridge . . . and on into the sea. If it had exploded it could hardly have failed to kill the captain, navigator, and gunnery lieutenant, and probably pretty well all the rest of us on both bridges. . . .

'We were rather in a mess for some minutes following that smash. But I remember that the officers, and especially the captain and navigator, were as cool as ice through it all. The captain went right on walking round the compass, taking his sights and giving his orders, while the "pilot" was squinting on top of the conning tower and following the *Emden* through his glasses just as though she had been a horse race. I even remember him finding time to laugh at me when I ducked as one or two of the first shells screamed . . .'

' "No use trying to get under the screen, Seabrooke— that canvas won't stop 'em!" '

The 6-inch shells of the *Sydney* whistled over the German. Glossop was having a hard time compensating for his damaged range-finder.

Now von Müller ordered course altered two points to starboard 'in order to obtain a more suitable range for our 10.5 centimetre guns, and to make it more difficult for the *Sydney* to keep on her mark.'

Suddenly, muffled cheers from the bridge of the *Emden*, as her officers spotted a flare-up of red flame from the after part of *Sydney*'s main deck, then boiling smoke.

Another lucky hit: this time on *Sydney*'s after control station, wounding or killing the entire crew. Once more the *Sydney* was seriously hampered in drawing 'bead' on the *Emden*. Gunners were compelled to fire by

[133]

the telescopes of each battery, an old-fashioned means of sighting, at best.

Emden's gunners were accurate. Another shell smashed through Glossop's cabin on the *Sydney* and opened a gash in the fo'c'sle. Watertight doors were dogged down in this critical area. Australian officers were already conceding.

'The *Emden* has the best of it!'

Von Müller knew he must manœuvre still closer. It was his only chance. Already the cruiser was battling at the outer limits of her guns' effective range.

Course was altered again to starboard. *Sydney*, aware of von Müller's tactics, pulled ahead as dense black smoke poured from her stacks. She was surging out of range like a race horse.

Emden's gunners, ramming home the heavy brass shells, fired, unloaded in a robot-like continuous motion. Momentarily, the after guns were silent, until *Emden*'s course change enabled them to bear once more.

Ears were deafened, eyes stung. One's whole being throbbed from the continual concussion.

Shells fell closer around the *Emden* . . . suddenly a blinding flash, a roar, and a searing, choking wave of heat. Men were thrown hard on to the decks, some never to rise again.

The German's fleet adversary had scored her first hit, on the fo'c'sle, just ahead of the conning tower. No. 1 gun was out of action.

The medical men ran out with stretchers, bandages and tourniquets. Some of the gunners were struggling up, on one knee, their faces, arms and bodies bloody.

Von Müller sized up the situation, realistically:

'As soon as the *Sydney* got our range a good deal of damage was done to the *Emden*, and this increased so quickly that I very soon got the impression that the *Sydney* had gained fire superiority over us.'

Another shell found its mark, exploding near the conning tower; it wounded Gaede, the gunnery officer, near the eye, Witthoeft, the torpedo officer on the chin and inflicted lesser cuts on other members of the crew.

The men looked at one another. Words were unnecessary. It was apparent *Sydney* had the range.

The speaking tube commenced to whistle . . . all orders would be transmitted by voice . . . the electric firing command system had been knocked out. It was often impossible to hear via the tube over din of battle; now, there was no choice.

Litter-bearers gathered up the dead and wounded from No. 1 gun. One seaman, his chest a clotted red mass, lay there on the stretcher, eyes staring in a strange look of surprise, rather than pain.

A sick berth attendant had collected a gory sack of arms and legs which he was dumping overboard.

The *Emden* suddenly reeled. She had been hit again. The alarm bells jangled wildly throughout her length— from a short circuit—until finally they were silenced.

The wireless cabin, and those on duty inside it, disappeared into sudden, almost unbelievable nothingness under the shock of a direct hit.

The helmsman was severely wounded in his left arm. He paled ashen grey, the blood spouted. His arm was bandaged and he stuck grimly to his post, turning the wheel, right, left, right, left. . . .

A shell landed just forward of the conning-tower, disabling the fo'c'sle gun-crews, along with two signalmen. First-aid parties were, for the moment, too busy elsewhere to come to the aid of those critically wounded.

Electric transmitters to the guns failed. Gunnery Officer Gaede had to pass his orders through speaking tubes. They, too, were being pierced with shrapnel and it was like trying to be heard at a distance by speaking through an elongated sieve, over the din of battle.

The brilliant shooting which had marked *Emden*'s opening salvoes was now out of the question. The guns remaining in action fired doggedly, desperately hoping only to keep in action.

Von Müller noted of this worsening phase:

'The steering-gear in the conning-tower went wrong at the same time as the helm-telegraph. Steering then had to be done from Section 1, orders being given to that section by speaking-tube. News came back to the conning-tower that the forward funnel had fallen over to port; and from another part (probably the poop) came the report that the guns were not getting enough ammunition.

'In order to get closer to the enemy and to obstruct his range-keeping I gave orders about fifteen minutes after the beginning of the fight to alter the course again two points to starboard, but changed this order before it was carried out to "one point to starboard", for the *Sydney*, owing to her superior speed, was already too far ahead of us, so that if I had made the greater turn, my after-guns would have been prevented from bearing.

'By splinters of a shell which exploded near the conning tower, the gunnery officer, Lieutenant Commander Gaede, was wounded near the eye; the torpedo officer (who was also acting as manœuvring officer) Lieutenant Witthoeft, was hit on the chin; and Ordinary Seaman Tietz, who was attending to the engine-room telegraph, and Ordnance Artificer Hartmann, who was transmitting orders to the guns, were slightly wounded. The last two had to leave the conning tower.

'About twenty minutes after the beginning of the fight, news came through from Section 1 that the steering-gear had gone wrong. What caused this failure of the steering gear I have never been able to ascertain. I ordered the hand-gear to be manned; accordingly, the navigating officer, Lieutenant-Commander Gropius, and the battle steersman, Able Seaman Busing, went aft to help the personnel of the after signal-station to get the hand-gear going.

'As nearly all the latter had been killed already, the personnel of the forward signal station—or those whose members of it had not been already put out of action— also went aft on to the poop; the hand-gear, however, could not be moved at all, evidently because its shafting had been jammed by a direct hit. Apparently the ammunition brought up for No. 4 gun had been blown up a little earlier by an enemy shell; besides other damage, this started a strong fire under the poop which made it impossible for the navigating officer and the personnel of the signal station to get back to Section 1. Lieutenant-Commander Gropius informed me that the hand-gear was unworkable, and then went aft again and helped to man No. 5 gun. . . .

'Meanwhile, the ship, because of the failure of the steering gear, had swung round about eight points to starboard; any further swing was checked by means of the screws. As the fire of our starboard guns had already weakened considerably, I did not alter her course again, but let the port battery come into action. From that time on, the ship was steered with the screws.

'During this phase of the fight, the range-finders failed. The fire of the port battery soon weakened also, probably because of the lack of ammunition and the serious casualties among the gun-crews and ammunition-carriers. The officer-in-charge of the range-finders, Sub-Lieutenant Zimmermann and Gunnery Mate von Risse, who had been engaged in transmitting orders, were sent aft to help the guns, as they were of no further use in the conning-tower.

'Both of these (men) were killed later in the course of the fight. From the torpedo room came the report that the torpedo-air-compressor was now out of action.'

As the battle went irrevocably against him, the imponderable decision mounted in critical import. Should he surrender, or continue battle on unequal terms, even though more men must be sacrificed?

In which course was duty, in which immortality . . . in which humanity, or cowardice? Where was the division line and who was to label it?

Indeed, was there any part of the training of a navy . . . other than accumulated years of experience and decisions on lesser planes of eminence . . . which enabled a commander to know the answer?

Had the *Emden* been at a greater weight disadvantage to the *Sydney* than its existing 2,000 tons, von Müller still would have had to accept battle. The *Mousquet* had the same decision to make at Penang.

With von Müller, as with all fighting men, though they may not discuss it, one of the complexes in determining a continuing action was that of shame. The fear of shame ranked in his mind even more poignantly than the fear of death.

At this maturing stage in his life, any course other than the one he pursued would have been unthinkable. Now, he did not have to harbour any apprehensions that he himself might do something ignoble.

Sydney was holding *Emden* off, as a long-armed boxer would a shorter opponent, whom he beats to a pulp at will. Some of the German cruiser's guns were manned now by only one man. The Chinese laundrymen cackled excitedly while passing ammunition:

'Maki-boom, maki-boom-boom . . . !' Their yellow skins glistened with sweat. They exhorted the gunners to make more 'boom!' for even they knew the tides of battle had left them in the ebb, already a broken piece of seemingly the sea's excrescence.

The surgery was fetid with the smells of death. The medical staff jabbed hypodermic after hypodermic into those who suffered the most acutely. Amputations were performed as a commonplace. Bloody rags littered the deck.

The wounded called out names of women, who could have been wives, mothers, sisters or sweethearts.

Every man, wounded or unscathed, thirsted desperately for water. But the tanks had been pierced with shrapnel and the supply of water had dwindled to a trickle. The sun beat cruelly down, the fires started by the exploding enemy shells raised the temperature to all but unbearable levels.

'By this time,' von Müller wrote, 'the prospect of getting within torpedo range of the enemy had become extremely small; still I did not wish to give up the attempt to attack with torpedoes, especially as the gunfight was going more and more against the *Emden*; I therefore put the ship to port against our opponent. When the distance had been decreased to about 4,900 yards, the *Sydney*, after making an unsuccessful attempt to torpedo us . . . swung sharply to starboard and stood away at high speed from the *Emden*. The gunnery officer, Lieutenant-Commander Gaede, who up till now had quietly controlled the gunfire under circumstances which were continually growing more difficult, now asked my permission to go down to the guns in order to put things right there, and proposed that I should continue to pass down the ranges to him. I agreed to do so. . . .'

Lieutenant von Hohenzollern himself recorded the bitter fight with undisguised dismay:

'The whole thing was now only a game for the enemy. The guns of the *Emden* no longer threatened, and the Englishman avoided a torpedo by steering a zig-zag course (our torpedo weapons were still intact). . . .

'Shortly afterwards, our Gunnery Officer left the conning-tower, as control from there had become impossible. He tried to get up a constant stream of fire again by bringing together all the survivors of the guns' crews and taking control himself from near the guns. He succeeded in manning two guns, but the effect of this last attempt was almost nothing, for the enemy kept at a safe distance, and maintained a steady fire on the vanquished *Emden*.

'The shells were hits, and again caused great losses and damage . . . another hit wrecked the captain's bridge . . . it was certain that our gunnery officer must be mortally wounded. Before, however, our Captain completely gave up the fight, he wished to make another attempt to get within torpedo range.

'This manœuvre was rendered more difficult by the fact that the communications between the conning-tower and the starboard engines had failed, and all orders had to be passed by a gunnery transmitter-man, who called the orders passed to him down the engine-room skylight. In spite of the hail of shells, orders were passed regularly, and the seaman concerned was not even slightly wounded.'

He was more fortunate than many of the wounded, who succumbed to fresh storms of shrapnel as they tried in vain to reach the dressing station.

On the stern, the fires raged. Some of the dead still lay on deck, bloody, scorched, like broken dolls in a maddened nursery. Others were splattered in pieces against the gun shields and bulkheads.

This was war. Here was no glory or stirring music— indeed the bandsmen themselves were too busy passing shell, projectiles and powder bags.

This was warfare at sea, attaining a new scientific perfection. The age of the high explosive cordite and lyddite shells had come into its own.

'Maki-boom . . . !' the Chinese laundrymen continued to urge. But no matter how much boom-boom the remaining guns might make, the lost shipmates could never be resummoned. They were expiring not in majesty as in a Wagnerian opera, but in dirty, infectious, stinking horror—in fear, and in indescribable pain.

These were the men, the children of fifteen or even ten years ago, who did not want to die. They cried in agony from their burns—but they wanted to live.

In the galley, the intense heat of the flames had melted glassware into crystal nuggets.

On to the deck fluttered keepsakes from the torn-open pockets of the men who would have use for them no more—wallets, lockets, photographs, with feminine writing scrawled across, 'With all my love . . .'

. . . on the stern, Gropius had all but abandoned attempts to get No. 5 gun back in action. In his ears von Müller's parting words rang, '*Gott mit Ihnen* . . . !'

Suddenly a flash, an eruption of a shell exploding under the torn deck . . . the navigating officer was blown into the air, engulfed in billowing grey smoke . . . when it cleared, there was not a trace of the officer, as though he had never existed at all other than as a figment in the fanciful minds of others.

Another lyddite shell blew into fragments near the mainmast, igniting a new cauldron of flame, angrily consuming more men. Von Müller was faced with the possibility that there would not be enough hands to man even his remaining guns.

He kept on his bridge, unwounded, relaying orders with grim impassiveness.

Surviving gunners hammered, pushed, even kicked at their damaged weapons to try to train them on the enemy. Skin rolled off their hands in strips, they bruised their knuckles and knees against the unyielding metal.

Men were trapped under portions of the *Emden*'s super-structure which had been blasted loose. A medical mate was making herculean efforts to dislodge a seaman from beneath the fallen funnel . . . there was scarcely time, or the tools to jack up the big, torn cylinder which was crushing his body.

Dense smoke and white steam clouds billowed from jagged holes in many parts of the hull. Magazines were menaced.

Hits were scoring repeatedly. There would be a flash, then concussion, a puff of smoke, sometimes a scream, or several—and new moans to be added to what was already a background dirge from the multitude of the mortally hurt.

The ship would stagger perceptibly under the heavier detonations, then miraculously shake herself, like a dog shakes itself, and continue the fight, reaching onward, onward over the ocean swells.

To many it seemed that the iron willpower of her captain alone kept *Emden* afloat and battling.

Word was passed that the fires were nearing the surgery. The doctors did not know how they could keep up with the increasing rate of the wounded. Oils and salves to treat the burn cases were being depleted.

Other men had inhaled too much smoke and they coughed and began to spit up blood. Still others were temporarily blinded by powder flashes close by their faces.

The whoom-whoom of the engines slowed. It was 10.45.

'The transmission of orders to the guns was now working very badly,' von Müller admitted, 'the speaking tubes being much damaged; the upper bridge had been shot away, the centre and after funnels knocked over, and the foremast went overside, carrying with it the Adjutant,

Sub-Lieutenant von Guerard, who had been stationed in the crow's nest as auxiliary observer for the guns, and Signalman Metzing.

'After the *Sydney* had fired its torpedo and turned away I wanted to make a second attempt to get within torpedo range of the enemy. I was not, however, able at first to send through the exchange to the starboard engine the order, "Stop the starboard screw! . . ."

'After some time, however, it again became possible, although with some delay, to send orders to the starboard engine. My order was "Everything you can get out of the engines!" But even at this second attempt my opponent would not let me get nearer than 5,500 or 6,000 yards.

'Our engines could now only attain a rate of a hundred-and-fifteen to one-hundred-and-twenty revolutions, which means a speed of nineteen-and-a-half knots, probably because the funnels had been shot away, and the furnace doors had, in consequence, to be left open to avoid danger from gas and smoke; further, one or two boilers had ceased functioning during the action.'

The situation in the engine-room was desperate. Ventilation had failed through the falling of the funnels, the stoppage of fans, and blowing in of the skylights. The steam and poisonous fumes more than once forced members of the staff to abandon their engine-room.

The *Emden* was being hit like a target in a shooting gallery. The decks were suffocating with flames and gases.

'We must make a hundred-and-twenty-five revolutions,' von Müller repeated, 'if we are to deliver our torpedoes.'

The schooner *Ayesha*

Von Muecke photographed with other survivors outside the Haidar Pasha
railway station in Constantinople

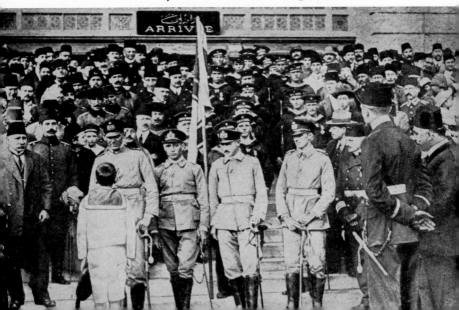

Lieutenant-Commander
Hellmuth von Muecke

Captain Karl von Müller

So the message orderly once again traversed the carnage of the deck, as shrapnel whistled past his ears to hit against steel with an ugly spat. He called the orders through the engine-room skylight and somehow made it back to the helm.

Something else, in addition to destruction of guns and gun-crews, was slowing down the fire—the ground swells. The *Sydney*'s 2,000-ton advantage afforded her added stability against the swells.

The engineers tried, but they could not deliver the r.p.ms. needed to close for a torpedo attack.

A stoker came on deck, as if to punctuate the death throes of the *Emden*'s engines. He was red-faced, half-scalded, panting for breath. But there was something even more remarkable about him—he was stark naked. Even his underwear had been blasted off.

'*Mein Gott, der Du bist im Himmel*,' he murmured. 'My Lord who is in Heaven.'

His body was burned saffron.

Then he sank to his knees, and died before anyone could help him.

A bos'n mate, his right arm shot away and blood spurting like a fountain, managed to get off one more round from his gun before he collapsed under the breech and expired.

A shell exploded in a pile of cordite. A more serious fire was averted by the bravery of a seaman who charged into the flaming mass and scattered it this way and that until the fires were out.

One shell had exploded inside the wardroom, where two cannon had been set up. Little remained of the guns or the men who had served them.

K   [145]

Adding to the labyrinthine chaos, coal had erupted from the bunkers to lie in dusty, shifting heaps everywhere. In areas where flames were not actually licking, the decks were so hot under foot as to be almost impassable.

It was 10.50, over an hour and a half since battle was joined. Steam hissed from a dozen ruptures in the engine piping and boilers. Yet *Emden* pushed on, up and over the ground swell, even though she was mortally hurt beyond any power of recall.

The torpedo room was a nightmare. Water, fire and smoke all vied in frightfulness to snatch the lives of those who remained inside.

Prince von Hohenzollern, with the assistance of the few men who were relatively unhurt, performed fast, heroic rescue work—pulling the men through the torpedo loading hatches and torpedo tubes. When the last men had been hauled to safety, he dogged down the metal covers to contain the flames.

Everywhere the young officer moved he saw death, suffering, holes in the steel plates, bent metal, burning rubbish and ashes . . . 'our once trim *Emden* was a ghastly sight!'

He heard moaning from almost every side, and when he investigated the fore battery, he discovered his gunnery officer.

'Gaede was lying at the port gun breathing his last breath,' the Prince recorded, 'dying fully conscious, for he still recognized me. His uniform was red with blood. He dozed while he was thanking me for the words of comfort I gave him, and was then carried on to the fo'c'sle where he soon afterwards closed his eyes for ever.

'His body was committed to the sea, according to seamen's custom.'

From Direction Island, on a vantage point, von Muecke was watching the death throes of the fight. He had returned with his raiding party to commandeer the ancient schooner.

'. . . I could at first see only the thick cloud of black smoke that the *Sydney*'s smoke stack was belching forth,' von Muecke said, 'but soon the masts, smoke stacks and upper deck came in sight. Of the *Emden* I could see only one smoke stack and one mast; the rest of the ship was below the horizon. Both cruisers were steering an easterly course, and both were still firing their guns.

'Suddenly at full speed the *Sydney* made a dash at the *Emden*. "Now," thought I, "the *Emden*'s last gun has been silenced, and the *Sydney* is running at her to deal her her death blow." But then, in the black smoke of the English ship, between the foremast and the nearest smoke stack, a tall column of water shot up, which could only be the result of a serious explosion. We supposed that it was caused by a well-aimed torpedo shot from the *Emden*.

'The *Sydney*, which was still running at a speed of twenty nautical miles, now made a quick turn to starboard, changed her course entirely and steamed slowly westward. The *Emden* continued to steer an easterly course. Both ships were still firing at each other, but the distance between them grew greater and greater until finally they were beyond reach of each other's guns.'

On the *Sydney*, Signalman Seabrooke had witnessed horror before the big cruiser had assumed a commanding offensive.

'. . . but the sight I shall never forget,' he wrote, 'was a whole body turning slowly in the air like a dummy in a cinema picture of an explosion. As the profile of the face showed sharp against the sky for an instant I recognized it as that of a chap who had been rather a pal of mine, and so I knew that poor old M—— had got his a couple of hours before I heard it from the surgeon.

'While I was edging along the deck with the stretcher party I saw out of the corner of my eye what appeared to be a funny sight—one of the gunners of S-2, which was not engaged at the time, dabbling his foot in a bucket of water. When I came back I saw it was anything but funny. Two of the crews of the starboard guns had been badly knocked about by the explosion of shells striking the deck at the end of their long high-angle flight. Among these was the chap I had seen apparently cooling his foot in a water-bucket. As a matter of fact it was no foot at all he was dabbing but only a maimed stump. The foot had been carried away by a shell fragment and the brave chap, not wanting to be put on the shelf by going down to the surgeon, had—all on his own—scooped up a canvas bucket full of salt water and was soaking his foot to stop the flow of blood.'

As the *Emden* reeled under her punishment the *Sydney*'s gunners found time to chalk-mark their shells with messages such as 'Cheerio,' 'Good Luck' and 'Kaiser'—proving to Seabrooke that '. . . they were a proper lot of "Don't-give-a-hangs" that crew!'

Soon, Seabrooke was recording in his notebook, like an excited angel of doom, the minute-by-minute death agonies of *Emden*:

'At 10.20 our lyddite caused a big explosion at the

[148]

foot of her mainmast, making a fire which never was entirely got under control.

'At 10.34 her foremast, and with it the fore-control, collapsed under a hard hit and disappeared over the far side.

'At 10.41 a heavy salvo struck her amidships, sending the second funnel after the first and starting a fierce fire in the engine-room. At 11.08 the third funnel went the way of the other two; and when I looked up from writing that down, I saw that the fore-bridge had done the disappearing act. . . .'

It was for history to decide whether von Müller had already let the carnage continue unnecessarily long, whether he had failed to make the point where valour became mortal stubbornness. Nonetheless, a few minutes after 11 a.m. the captain of the *Emden* noted:

'. . . our gunfire had completely collapsed, so I swung away from the *Sydney* by stopping the starboard engine. Shortly afterwards I was informed from the torpedo room that it must be abandoned on account of a leak from a shot under water . . . as it was now impossible for me to damage my opponent in any way further, I decided to put my ship, which was badly damaged by gunfire and burning in many places, on the reef in the surf of the weather-side of North Keeling Island and to wreck it thoroughly in order not to sacrifice needlessly the lives of the survivors.'

Von Müller, who had endured more than should be expected of human nerves, conceded that the possibility of miracles was past. Nothing would enable *Emden* to make 'Boom-boom!' any more . . . never.

To Witthoeft, he said:

'Witthoeft, this is it. I must save the people—the people, Witthoeft!'

He ordered all possible speed, and the engineers squeezed nearly nineteen knots out of the dying engines. The burning cruiser shook throughout her tortured, jagged length as she rushed towards that palm-fringed crescent of coral, North Keeling Island, sixteen miles north-west of the main Cocos group.

Even so, the *Sydney* remained a grey, implacable nemesis. Recognizing the intent of her vanquished foe, she redoubled her fury . . . not wishing to let *Emden* beach herself and thereby avoid being sunk. The *Sydney* wanted this 'honour', to complete the task of destruction which she had begun, as though the shell-racked little cruiser symbolized a waterborne Carthage.

The Australian increased her fire rate, pumping an avalanche of shells at the *Emden*. She put up her speed and cut across the bows of von Müller's command, in an effort to head her off from the island.

One port gun of *Emden* was able to bear on *Sydney* and fire as she streaked past. It was as futile as a pop-gun. A rumbling new salvo from *Sydney* killed more men on the decks of the German.

The *Sydney* abandoned her attempts to intercept, perhaps, fearing a torpedo, being rammed or even running aground.

The palm trees towered higher, the beach stretched white and inviting. The crew, on this little island, could obtain coconuts and drink the milk before they went mad from thirst. There would also be gull eggs for food.

Now the distance was 300 yards, 200 . . . 100 . . .

It was exactly 11.15 a.m., November 9th, 1914.

A jar, a jolting, abrupt impact. Von Müller was thrown against the bulkhead, on to the deck. Everyone else at the control station was down. The helm itself was bent like a bow by the impact.

The engines had ceased. All became suddenly, unnaturally quiet, and motionless. It was journey's end.

. . . these were the Cocos, which might have been a million miles away from Blankenburg and the life that von Müller, and his men, knew.

Emden, a blasted steel coffin, was hard aground. But, inconceivable as it seemed, the battle was not over.

CHAPTER 12

MEANWHILE, von Muecke was busily readying *Ayesha* for sea, not only to spare his men prisoner-of-war camp, but to frustrate, if he could, the Australians in their moment of victory.

He had collected firearms from the English cable and wireless station operators, raised the German flag over Direction Island and declared martial law in effect. He had prepared to defend the island if the cruiser sent a landing party ashore . . . and gave permission to the civilians to leave for another island in case a fight broke out.

'Accompanied by two of my signalmen,' he wrote, 'I now took my station on the roof of the highest house to watch the fight between the two cruisers. As a whole, the Englishmen showed little interest in the conflict that was going on but a few thousand metres distant from the island. Other matters seemed to claim their attention. With an ingratiating smile one of them stepped up to our officers, who were head over ears in work down on the beach, and asked:

' "Do you play tennis?"

'. . . the point for me to settle now was what to do with the landing squad. So far as our ship was concerned, the damage she had suffered at the hands of a far superior foe was so great that a return to the island, even in the event of a most favourable outcome of the battle, was out of the question. She must run for the nearest port where she could make repairs, bury her dead, and leave her wounded. At the same time I could count with certainty upon the arrival of an English war vessel before long in Keeling harbour, to learn what had happened to the cable and wireless station. For, had not the telegraphic service to Australia, Batavia and Mauritius been cut off entirely?

'With our four machine-guns and twenty-nine rifles we could, for the time at least, have prevented the English from making a landing on the island, but against the fire of the English cruiser's heavy guns, which would then have been directed against us, we would have had no defence whatever. Taking everything into consideration, therefore, we could do no more than defer the surrender of a position that, from the outset, it had been impossible to hold. Moreover, confinement in an English prison was little to our taste.

'Now, fortunately for us, the small white schooner that we had failed to blow up was still riding at anchor in the harbour. It could, and it should, help us to escape from our predicament. I decided to leave the island on the little boat. Her name was *Ayesha* and at one time she had served to carry copra from Keeling to Batavia two or three times a year, and to bring provisions back with her on her return trip. Now that steamship service had been established between these two points, she lay idle and dismantled in the harbour, and was gradually falling into decay.

'Taking no one with me, I got into the steam launch and went out to the schooner to learn whether she was at all seaworthy. The captain and a single sailor were aboard her. Of the former I inquired casually whether he had any ammunition aboard, for I did not wish him to suspect the real purpose of my coming. He said there was none, and a brief inspection of the ship led me to believe that she was still seaworthy. Consequently I sent my officers and men aboard the *Ayesha* to get her into trim for sailing.

'There was plenty to do on the little ship. All the sails and rigging had been taken down and stowed away, and had now to be put in place again.

'When the Englishmen on the island realized that it was my intention to sail off in the schooner, they warned me with great earnestness against trusting ourselves to her, saying that the *Ayesha* was old and rotten and could not stand a sea voyage. Furthermore, they informed me that an English warship, the *Minotaur*, and a Japanese cruiser were in the vicinity of the island and that we would surely fall a prey to one of them.

'As my predecessor in command of the *Ayesha* was leaving her, he wished me God-speed and concluded with the comforting remark, "But the ship's bottom is worn through."

'When, in spite of all these warnings, we remained firm in our purpose, and continued the work of getting the *Ayesha* ready for sea, the sporting side of the situation began to appeal to the Englishmen, and they almost ran their legs off in their eagerness to help us. Could it have been gratitude that impelled them to lend us their aid? It is a question I have never been able to answer to my satisfaction, although, to be sure, several of them did express a feeling of relief at the thought that now the fatiguing telegraph service with its many hours of overwork and its lack of diversion was a thing of the past. They showed us where the provisions and water were kept, and urgently advised us to take provisions from the one side, where they were new and fresh, rather than from the other, where they were stale. They fetched out cooking utensils, water, barrels of petroleum, old clothes, blankets and the like, and themselves loaded them on trucks and brought them to us. From every side, invitations to dinner poured down upon us; my men were supplied with pipes and tobacco; in short, the Englishmen did all they could to help us out.

'Nor were they sparing with advice as to the course we ought to take, and time proved that all they told us of wind and weather, of currents, etc. was in every way trustworthy. As the last of our boats left the shore, the Englishmen gave us three hearty cheers, wished us a safe journey, and expressed their gratitude for the "moderation" which we had shown in the discharge of our duty, wherein all of our men had behaved "generously", they said. Then, cameras in hand, they still swarmed about the *Ayesha*, taking pictures of her . . .'

Superintendent Farrant, when the Germans left, together with his staff, 'groped for and dug up our buried mirror, collected cells from the various hiding places in the bush and quickly got into communication with Batavia, who answered our second or third short call . . .'

Von Muecke's report was little exaggerated. As a matter of fact, the cable and wireless personnel were almost sorry to see the Germans go. Companionship, new faces, and certainly tennis matches, were not commonplace on their pin-point of coral in the Indian Ocean.

And on the *Emden*, von Müller regained his feet after he had directed his ship on to the coral reef.

'Full speed ahead!' he ordered.

Suggestions of blood streaked his face and hands. He was smudged, his uniform torn.

But 'full speed' wasn't electrifying any more. The grounded hulk strained and quivered. Steam and pungent, poisonous smoke poured through the jagged metal wounds amidships which led to the charred world of the engines. The cruiser could not be impaled more firmly.

'Stop!' was his next order. The grinding noise from the damaged and heat-warped machinery ceased again . . . once more quiet as a grave save for the crackling of the fires aft and the softer, but obtruding groans of the wounded and dying.

'Open all sea-cocks and draw the fires!' von Müller ordered. It was his last involving the operation of his ship.

A shell whistled close by, hit with a splat and a geyser of sand on the beach a hundred yards off the bow. Another smashed into the fo'c'sle head, which resembled a junk yard. It sent the maze of broken anchor chain once more flying and clanking about the serrated decking.

'Tell all hands they have my permission to jump overboard and save themselves!' von Müller passed the new order. But the current was swirling swift and treacherous around the sides.

The firing continued from the *Sydney* circling to port. *Emden* could not fire back. She was a burning hulk.

Some of the men did jump into the waters, which promised more of a sanctuary than the deathly target of

[157]

their ship. One or two vanished, struggling, beneath the surface.

By the time the order was fully passed to open sea-cocks, the firing ceased. It was 11.20.

There was a darkening smudge of smoke pouring from the *Sydney* as she streaked away to find the *Buresk*.

Magazines were flooded, what few guns remained serviceable were put out of action. This was accomplished by throwing breech-blocks overboard and destroying the optical sights. Witthoeft was scuttling the torpedo director, and von Müller personally was burning and tossing into the sea, one by one, code books, log—all secret documents.

It was a sad duty, completing the destruction which the *Sydney* had started.

There were many, many other tasks to be tended to. The wounded—what to be done with them?

Existence below decks had become impossible. The surgery was an odorous, smouldering charnel house. All the patients were being carried up on deck and into the air. The weakest were covered with hammocks against the beating sun.

Those who had already succumbed had to be abandoned to the ever-creeping flames, which moved forward from the cauldron of the stern. At that, it was better commitment than the sea—already the knifing fin, the sudden splash, as a shark attacked a floating corpse. Giant crabs would be waiting on the sea bottom.

A gruesome, but nonetheless pressing problem was thereby accentuated. What to do with those who had not found their own fiery tomb inside the ship? Surely they could not be left on deck under the scorching sun.

The dead were everywhere. Among their pitiful number were the Chinese laundrymen, like torn and discarded toys. As von Hohenzollern recorded:

'The two Chinese lay, like many of our gallant men, dead on the spot where they had expired in the execution of their duty . . .'

Never more would they exhort, 'Maki-boom-boom!'

Nor would von Müller ever be able to ask:

'Nothing new, Mr. Gropius?'

Or, to his gunnery officer:

'Gaede, everything in order?'

. . . von Hohenzollern continued:

'As there were many severely wounded men lying about the ship, I and a few men tried to get aft from the waist, between the decks. We could not, however, get farther than the engine-room hatch. The heat aft was still so great, and the metal was still glowing in such a way, that to enter would have resulted in severe burns.

'Everything looked very bad there. A hit had pierced the side of the upper coal bunker in the gangway, and the whole of the coal had rolled into the gangway and almost completely blocked it. There was nothing to be done, but to creep over the coal.

'We tried to get farther aft, but had to give up and return to the fore part of the ship on account of the unbearable heat, glowing metal, and the water which had quickly run in. We discovered a few wounded, however, and brought them up to the others.

'In the meantime all the severely wounded men had been brought on to the fo'c'sle. Bandages were applied as far as they would go. As they did not last out we took the bed-linen and table-cloths, which were of good linen and did very good service.

'A few men had availed themselves of the permission to swim to the island. The attempt looked easier than it was. The difficulty was the very heavy surf. It fell on the reef with colossal force, and many men had their heads dashed on the coral and lost their lives. In spite of their physical strength this fate was shared by Assistant-Doctor Schwabe.'

Men stood by the twisted rails, breathing hard, trying to rid their lungs of the noxious coal gases, while staring in a dazed stupor. The wreck of the ship, their dead comrades, the end seemingly of everything—all of these shocks to the mind contained the germ of madness, a germ which perhaps would have grown had the numbness of complete exhaustion not acted as an antidote.

Von Müller, his shirt sleeves rolled, now had finished the destruction of his secret papers. He was busy checking the wounded. It was obvious to him that many of them, perhaps even the majority, would die before another sun rose.

He paused beside one badly hurt seaman and asked how he felt. He put his hand lightly on the man's head.

'I think I am going to be all right,' he answered, then asked, '*Herr Kapitän*, are we going to go home soon?'

'Yes, my young man,' von Müller replied.

Before von Müller could say anything more, the man turned his head to the side and appeared to go limp. In a very few minutes he, too, was committed to the swirling seas.

Drinking water mounted almost by the minute as a

critical problem. Whether or not there were fresh pools on North Keeling Island, the milk from coconuts, in which the atoll abounded, would assuage thirsts. Every man knew that. Some of the wounded, even those with hurts less than mortal, could only lie beneath their hammock and canvas sun-shelters and repeat in gasping monotony:

'*Wasser, Wasser . . . bitte, Wasser. . . .*'

It was suggested that a line be floated ashore, using a drum, breeches-buoy, planking, anything that might tow a heavy hawser along with it.

Several attempts at this seemingly logical way of linking with the land failed. The floats swirled out and then would double back around the other side of the *Emden* . . . or they would drift in swiftly to shore only to snag hopelessly on the bordering coral rocks which fringed the beach and cruelly frustrate hopes.

Von Müller, topsides again, clenched and unclenched his fists helplessly. He, of all people, would be the last to give voice to his feelings. The disappointment was almost too bitter to bear, beaten, soul-weary and sick to the core as most were.

'Can't anyone get a line to land?' was the unspoken question on von Müller's lips.

The surf swirled around the cruiser's torn sides and splashed a mocking tattoo. The sun danced off spray flecks.

One seaman, seized with an impulse, stripped off his smudged, ripped khaki trousers, and kicked his shoes into the sea. The blistering deck singed the soles of his feet. He clutched the end of a coil of rope and dived over.

Half an hour later he was hauled aboard, gasping a

L

fantastic tale. It had been at first a pleasant experience, swimming shoreward in the swift, blandishingly warm waters . . . they had an antiseptic quality to his blistered skin, even to his parched tongue. He drank in the salty liquid as he stroked.

The men-o'-war birds began to circle overhead, lower and lower. Suddenly a strange thing happened. They attacked him, like vampires. They squawked and dived at his eyes with their sharp beaks.

He tugged at his line, but the men holding it on the ship could not feel his signalling. He beat the birds off with his fists and swore at them, using every curse and epithet that ever echoed from a Wilhelmshaven sailor bar.

As they had appeared, they vanished again . . . in the direction of some floating object thirty yards away from him. A floating corpse perhaps.

He had come close to the beckoning sands of the beach, and the waving green palm fronds, when his line snagged on the reef. He could go neither forward nor back. If he let go he might be dashed by the combers on to the jagged coral. He might also be tossed up, alive, on to North Keeling, alone—to starve to death. He had visions of the birds picking his flesh clean, his bones bleaching white under the tropical sun.

But the water was soft, caressing, and he almost drifted off in pleasant reverie, as his thoughts returned to Germany, the dog-drawn milk carts in the morning, the sound of the policeman's footsteps at night and of his village. He was brought back to reality, first by violent cramps in his stomach and the awareness of pain from a swollen tongue—the reward for gulping salt water.

And as he looked about, he saw the shark sweeping with the certainty of doom toward him. A splash, the 'V' of the monster's tail flipping up, then under with brutal speed, a rush of water . . . he figured he was done for . . . his body strained against the rope.

Several yards away, the shark struck . . . and the birds screeched and flapped into the air as the creature stole their prey.

The sailor hauled himself along the line, foot by foot, through the boiling surf. When he was only yards from the *Emden* the fin reappeared, knifing behind him . . . almost too close to escape this time . . . then a mighty heave, and he was pulled out of the water and on to the deck of the cruiser, just as the ugly tail flayed the air and hurtled beneath the surface. The razor-teeth closed on empty water.

He was safe. He lay on the deck, gasping for breath.

Among the pitiful multitude of the wounded were several who had been even less fortunate than their shipmate. They had been smashed against the barnacled plates of the *Emden* or the reefs, and had sustained skull fractures, deep lacerations.

The area that was in any way habitable had shrunk to the narrow confines of the fo'c'sle, hot and littered with the battle's debris as it was. However, it was at the furthest distance from the burning stern.

Soon, another problem was added to the Calvary of the afternoon—the gulls now were trying to attack all of the wounded, even as they had the lone swimmer. Men had to stand watch with sticks and pistols to fight off the hideous winged creatures.

Morphine was gone, and the lack of water remained a

threat to continued existence. Before the eyes of almost everyone swam taunting images of crystal clear pools and cool waterfalls.

'*Wasser, bitte. . . .*'

The afternoon went, without water, without food, without a line having been floated ashore . . . without any real hope. The wounded died, one by one, and had to be committed. Throats were so parched that the officers could hardly murmur even a prayer. The creatures of the sea waited, just below the beguilingly calm surface.

Existence had become a hell on earth that no one ever had anticipated would be his lot.

. . . during this time the *Sydney* had overhauled the *Buresk*. Lieutenant-Commander Klopper, in charge of the latter's prize crew, ordered that she be scuttled at once. She had already stopped dead in the water at the *Sydney*'s challenge.

Klopper blew up the wireless shack and burned his papers. The German crew set to work to provision life-boats—in the event the *Sydney* had no accommodation for them.

The *Sydney*, recognizing these scuttling operations, fired a shot over the *Buresk*'s bow. Klopper signalled:

'There are Englishmen on board.'

There was no further shooting.

'Open the Kingston valves . . . speed the scuttling!' Klopper ordered from the navigation bridge. He smiled at the thought that the remaining English crew consisted of only a steward and a cook. The others had long since been sent to a neutral port.

'Haul down your flag!' the *Sydney* now ordered.

The German flag was hauled down, weighted and thrown overboard.

Within half an hour a cutter containing an armed prize crew from the *Sydney* came alongside, and ordered the *Buresk* to follow the Australian to the *Emden*. She was to take aboard the German survivors.

'Our boilers have been blown out, the engine-room is flooded . . . we are sinking,' Klopper replied succinctly.

This angered the Australians, but there was obviously nothing to be done. The *Buresk*'s crew took to the boats and were led over to the *Sydney*.

Captain Glossop turned towards Direction Island, watching with a certain frustration, the *Buresk*'s bow slowly sinking astern.

On the *Emden* some of the men had sufficiently recovered their breath and their strength for another try at running a line ashore.

Two of the *Emden*'s most powerful swimmers now went over. One vanished in the surf on the leeward side of the reef, the other was pulled back aboard.

The survivors became resigned to waiting on the wreck for the *Sydney* to pick them off—*if* she were to return.

Already the sun was past the zenith and slanting westward. The broiling attrition of its rays was diminishing.

'About 4 p.m. the *Sydney* was again sighted to the westward,' von Müller wrote. 'As she had two boats in tow, we imagined that she intended taking the survivors on board. When a fairly long distance from the *Emden*, the boats were cast loose, and the *Sydney* steamed past the *Emden*'s stern at a distance of about 4,300 yards . . .'

. . . these were the boats from the scuttled *Buresk*

and the *Emden*'s sailors brightened perceptibly as the warship cleaved the flat afternoon waters. Even prospects of an English prison were attractive.

'. . . as she had international signals flying I sent a Morse message by flag:

' "No signal-book aboard!" . . . for our signal-book had been burnt.'

The *Sydney* dipped its flag hoist, which read, 'Do you surrender?' and raised it again.

Captain Glossop decided to reopen the battle.

Signalman Seabrooke was at the side of Glossop.

'We were at fairly close range,' he recalled, 'and I heard Lieutenant R. ask the captain what part of the ship he should direct his fire upon. The captain studied the *Emden* through his glass for a few moments and then, remarking that most of the men appeared to be bunched at opposite ends of the ship—on the fo'c'sle and quarter-deck—said he thought that there would be less chance of killing anyone if the fire was directed somewhere between those two points.

'Then I heard him give the definite order:

' "Open fire and aim for foot of mainmast!" '

Captain Glossop later explained, 'I hated to do it, it makes me feel almost a murderer. Since my question, "Do you surrender?" went unanswered I assumed the *Emden* wanted to continue the fight.'

What he left unsaid might have been psychologically closer to the reason: that, considering the reputation the *Emden* had gained as an invincible, wily foe, no one, not even John Glossop, could believe she was an impotent hulk.

Grey-black smoke lay aft on her wake as the relatively

unharmed *Sydney* boiled back into the attack—but it was to be one of history's strangest, and most tragic, naval actions. Its adversary was plainly a blackened heap of metal.

'. . . when the *Sydney* had passed our stern and lay aft on our starboard quarter, she opened fire again unexpectedly with several salvoes. . . .'

A white puff from a fore gun of the mighty *Sydney*, another from an aft battery. Von Müller and all who still lived on the *Emden* gaped in disbelief . . . in the next second the all-too-familiar banging overhead as a shell streaked above the remains of the cruiser towards North Keeling Island . . . men-o'-war birds, which had continued to hover raucously over the wounded, flapped away.

The second shell hit amidships. A stoker who had been watching beside von Hohenzollern, collapsed with little commotion, like a clay figure in a shooting gallery.

He sprawled on the deck, a look of bewilderment on his dead, ashen face.

Von Müller repeated his earlier order:

'Whoever can swim may jump overboard if he wishes!'

'They are killing us with a dog's meanness!' an officer exclaimed. The same officer, mollified by time, said later, 'The second shelling was caused by some misunderstanding and, perhaps, some nervousness on Captain Glossop's side.'

One sailor, in a gesture of supreme desperation, snatched up a rifle and fired a clip of bullets at the speeding *Sydney*. It was as futile as aiming a slingshot at the cruiser.

Fresh fires were started. Plates were torn anew.

Sailors began to jump into the eddying, shark-infested waters.

Suddenly, von Müller's cabin servant, a piece of white linen in hand, jumped on to the tilting, shell-scarred mainmast and started up, like a boy shinnying up a tree on a summer's afternoon.

His shipmates watched agape. The shells continued to hammer in, and explode in their own shattering omega of existence.

Now, he had torn the German ensign off the peak and fastened the white linen in its place. He slid down, to safety.

Cheers went up.

Salvoes all at once ceased. The echoes reverberated through the island vegetation . . . faded into silence until there was only the lap of water against the sides of the wrecked *Emden* and, always, the moan of the critically wounded.

'. . . a number of the crew went overboard; some reached the island, some were drowned in the attempt (among them the capable Torpedo-Machinist Pyttlik), some were afterwards dragged back on board. . . .'

With the additional casualties, the *Emden* had now lost almost half her personnel. And her original complement of about three hundred and twenty was further depleted by the absence of the raiding party on Direction Island.

Von Müller ordered the flag burnt, as a final proof of submission and degradation. He watched the flames consume the cloth, watched until the sparkling colours and the bunting had melted into brittle carbon shell.

Then the shell, too, crumbled. Only ashes remained.

Von Müller turned away, not wanting to speak, not wanting to look at anyone.

There could be no doubt now on the *Sydney*, that the *Emden* had surrendered. The battle, at last, was at an end.

Later, von Müller commented on Glossop's reasoning that *Emden* wished to continue the fight:

'This explanation cannot be considered a very sound one when one remembers that the *Emden* during the last phase of the fight had been unable to fire her guns any more, that she was lying a wreck on the reef, and that by her signal "No Signal-book aboard" it was implied that she was ready to negotiate. I can, I think, say that in his place I should not have behaved so, but that I should have sent a boat to the *Emden*, probably under a flag of truce. . . .'

The *Sydney* steamed off towards the main Cocos group, intending to recapture Direction Island. One of the boats from the *Buresk* was sent to the *Emden*, with the message the *Sydney* would return the next day.

The *Emden*'s survivors had learned the meaning of total, punishing defeat, of utter exhaustion of mind and body. Some stood and stared like ghosts. Others lay on their backs, mouths open, gasping for breath as though their lungs would burst; among them were the drenched survivors of the last group to jump overboard.

On the mastpeak an alphabet flag flew upside down—international signal of distress. It bespoke anew the death which had come to stay as an unwelcome brother.

The afternoon passed in a mixed miasma of sound—muted suffering, the sounds of death—and of pulsing, unreal sights, and of stifling smells. It was world's end to those who inhabited this microscopic cosmos.

Fevers rose and pain in scores of bodies throbbed into full insistence, acutely dominating consciousness.

'*Mein Gott . . . mein Gott . . . !*' but those who implored the Lord were too mortally hurt to recite a full prayer or even to mumble a hymn.

At dusk the birds left. The glow from the sun persisted in the west like an ugly, sultry sore that was reluctant to be blotted into nothingness.

Fires broke out anew. Lieutenant Fikentscher and other Germans from the late prize crew of the *Buresk* were now aboard and lent their fresh energies to combating the flames.

Still there was no food, no water . . . and no one, not even the powerful swimmers, dared answer again the Lorelei beckoning of North Keeling's close shores.

Adding to the horror, officers and men commenced to find their old shipmates.

'I did not wish to miss an opportunity of looking for my friend Levetzow,' von Hohenzollern, for one, recalled. 'Near the mainmast I discovered his remains. There were only bones; the rest was burnt. From the shape of the head and an Oberleutnant's star I was certain that it was really Levetzow. He must have been killed by the explosion of the ammunition for the after battery. His remains were committed to the sea. . . .'

It was hardly the kind of war comprehensible to the people who would wave flags in rhythm to band music as they watched soldiers march in Unter den Linden, or the Champs Elysées, or the Mall, or even Pennsylvania Avenue.

The ship, impaled and consumed beyond any possibility of salvage, remained hot, like some eternal oven of the nether regions, and nowhere was there water. Men climbed gingerly overboard, hanging on to rope ladders, to try vainly to satisfy a thirst which could not be assuaged. Others scooped up sea water in canvas buckets, drank the burning, salty contents only to vomit it up . . . but nonetheless to gulp again in their nearly insane craving.

'*Wasser* . . . *Wasser*. . . .' It was a refrain from purgatory which none who heard it that long, fearsome night could ever, ever forget. Darkness fell. The Southern Cross appeared overhead. The living night sounds began to whisper in tropical *obbligato* from the depths of the island, lulling somehow the refrain of misery that even the gutted vitals of the blackened cruiser seemed to emit.

Night, finally cloaked the survivors in their anguish, as under an immense shroud. It brought peace— sepulchral and restive, but nonetheless peace.

It did, to those save the seriously wounded, and a captain named Karl von Müller.

CHAPTER 13

BETWEEN the Cocos Islands and the British Isles lies some 10,000 miles of land and water, ten hours difference in point of time. Before noon on that same fateful November 9th, there was history of its own to be made in Lloyd's insurance office. As reported in a London dispatch to the *New York Times*:

The business of the day was in full swing, when suddenly above the hum, the Lutine bell rang out. Only on momentous occasions is this bell rung.

Instantly business was suspended and all turned toward the rostrum, from which it was known that some great news was to be made public. The official crier mounted the steps and, in the rolling tones for which he is famous, began: 'Gentlemen, it is officially announced that the *Emden*——'

That is as far as he was allowed to go. Cheer after cheer went up. Hats and papers were thrown into the air.

Again the Lutine bell was rung, to enjoin silence —and at last the message was completed that the *Emden* had been destroyed.

The shipping industry in the Indian Ocean is now relieved of the greater portion of its peril and underwriters will sleep more comfortably. It is perhaps no exaggeration to say that this ship alone has inflicted more damage to British merchant shipping than all the rest of the German Navy combined.

Editorial writers in the same seat of Empire were penning their own tributes. The London *Daily Telegraph* admitted:

It is almost in our heart to regret that the *Emden* has been captured or destroyed. . . . He (von Müller) has been enterprising, cool and daring in making war on our shipping, and has revealed a nice sense of humour. He has, moreover, shown every possible consideration to the crews of his prizes. So far as is known, he destroyed over 74,000 tons of shipping without the loss of a single life. There is not a survivor who does not speak well of this young German, the officers under him and the crew obedient to his orders. The war on the sea will lose something of its piquancy, its humour and its interest now that the *Emden* has gone.

And the London *Daily Chronicle* opined that von Müller:

. . . handled his ship with the skill of an accomplished sea officer and the courtesy of a chivalrous gentleman. He has been an ornament to the sea profession and an honour to the brotherhood of the sea.

From the other side of the Atlantic, the *New York Times*:

. . . the extraordinary skill, audacity and heroism of the *Emden*'s officers and men will not soon be forgotten. She was no privateer out for booty but a ship of the German Navy fighting for the German people. . . . She had no harbour or refuge.

The *Scientific American*, assessing later the artillery aspects of the fight, expressed constrained horror at the 'frightful execution which well-directed shell fire can do upon the hull, decks and superstructure of a light cruiser.'

The German press went to understandable lengths of eulogy. The Kaiser himself telegraphed the namesake city of the *Emden* to promise:

'A new and stronger *Emden* shall arise, on whose bow the Iron Cross shall be affixed in remembrance of the old *Emden*.'

Sydney, Australia, meanwhile, thinking the German survivors would be brought 'down under', commenced unheard-of preparations to welcome von Müller comparable to a Broadway ticker-tape parade. His glory even over-shadowed their own Captain Glossop.

Friend or foe, the nations of the world were strangely humble in tribute to a man whose conduct was almost archaic by the stark new standards of the Twentieth Century. In warfare, he had proven himself almost the last of another generation, which put decency and humanity above all else.

His British foes sincerely meant all they said of him.

For Karl von Müller the war was over, but it was to be a long journey home. Nor, in fact, was this lonely commander ever, on the whole broad earth, to find the soul's peace which he so rightfully deserved.

Captain Glossop insisted that von Müller keep his

sword. The latter smiled at this final irony. On a ship like the *Emden* there had been no room for swords.

'On November 11th,' Captain von Müller wrote, '. . . the *Sydney* proceeded to Colombo. The treatment of the prisoners of war aboard her was good and I must particularly recognize the great care that was taken of the wounded and some of the unwounded who were trans-shipped to the auxiliary cruiser *Empress of Russia* in order to make room on the *Sydney*.

'On the 15th the *Sydney* reached Colombo where all the wounded were landed and placed in hospital, and all the other survivors of the *Emden*'s crew were distributed among various steamers of the convoy to be taken to Malta.'

Witthoeft said:

'The treatment which we received aboard the Australian cruiser was unquestionably good . . . both the doctors and their attached personnel wore themselves almost to the bone.'

En route to Colombo, Sub-Lieutenant Stoffers, a petty officer and two men died of their wounds. The complement of the *Emden* seemed to be shrinking into relative nothingness.

Warships which had figured in *Emden*'s spectacular but brief career were encountered again: the *Hampshire*, convoying the *Empress of Russia* through to Suez, and the *Dupleix* and *Montcalm*, at anchor off Port Said. At the latter port the officers of the *Emden* were allowed to buy civilian clothes and warm coats, while the sailors were fitted out in English Naval uniforms.

Early in December, the *Emden* survivors reached journey's end, at Malta, in the Mediterranean. The old fort, known as Verdala Barracks, was to be home for many months.

Von Müller was assigned to a room by himself. On one of the first nights there he was surprised by a chorusing outside his window. The serenade ended with 'Deutschland über Alles', as the singers' eyes moistened.

Other prisoners of war, German and Austrian merchant marine personnel and enemy civilians, were serenading him. Long before his arrival, von Müller had become a legend.

The months wore on, and the prisoners were treated correctly but with austerity. Von Müller worked unceasingly to obtain privileges for his command: more exercise space, more food, better medical care, better insect and rodent control. An army of bed bugs increased in force, and ferocity, until some nights, the men joked bitterly, they would have carried off the metal cots had they not been fastened to the floors.

Baths must be paid for and there was insufficient heat to keep out the wintry gales that swept across the eastern reaches of the Mediterranean. There were few electric lights, a lack that the ration of one candle a week per man did little to compensate. Nonetheless, von Müller sat up night after night, straining his eyes as he wrote his report, taking his mind temporarily away from the terrible hours off the Cocos:

'Condition of the crew who were in the fight: (a) killed, drowned or succumbed to their wounds after the fight, 7 officers, 1 staff paymaster, 4 warrant officers, 25 petty officers, 92 men, 1 civilian cook, 1 barber, and 3 Chinese laundrymen; (b) severely wounded, 1 warrant officer, 3 petty officers, 17 men; (c) slightly wounded,

2 officers, 2 warrant officers, 9 petty officers, 31 men; (*d*) unwounded, 6 officers, 5 warrant officers, 39 petty officers, 67 men. The losses were especially heavy among the gun-crews and the ammunition-carriers. I think I may state definitely that in this action, which unfortunately led to the destruction of His Imperial Majesty's ship, *Emden*, every one of the officers, warrant officers, petty officers and men under my command did his duty.

'During her three months' cruise the *Emden*'s engines had made 10,000,000 revolutions, representing a course of 30,000 miles. By the good work of the engine-room crew and stokers under the able leadership of Engineer-Lieutenant Ellerbrock, who was effectively seconded by Engineer Sub-Lieutenant Stoffers for the main engines, and Engineer Sub-Lieutenant Haas for the boilers—serious troubles were avoided, and even minor mishaps were very few in number . . .'

He wrote on, detailing the cruise of the raider. It was from memory since he had destroyed all log books.

Mail was slow in arriving, and in being sent on its way. But newspapers were plentiful, and von Müller was kept well apprised of the fluctuating fortunes of war. He read successively of such developments as:

The loss of von Spee and virtually his entire squadron in an engagement off the Falkland Islands.

The carnage at Gallipoli—there the troops of the Australian convoy escorted by the *Sydney* proved anew, even as had the *Emden*, that a kind of victory can still be realized in what to all appearances is sanguinary defeat.

The sinking (by Walther Schwieger of the U-20, a naval acquaintance of von Müller's) of the huge

Cunarder *Lusitania*, with a loss of nearly 1,200 lives, including Americans. Not even von Müller could have estimated at that time the effect this single torpedoing was to have on the war's outcome.

The execution in Brussels of a British nurse named Edith Cavell. She had harboured enemy soldiers in her hospital. Neither could this be fully appreciated at the time in all its emotional dimensions. In effect, it was to prove a worse defeat for the Kaiser than the loss of von Spee's Squadron—or of the subsequent attrition at Jutland, including eleven major fighting ships of the High Seas Fleet.

The loss of the *Hampshire*, with War Secretary Lord Kitchener aboard . . . and, in April, 1917, the entry of America into the conflict. It had happened on a Good Friday and the news arrived officially among the Malta prisoners Easter Monday. Von Müller could only read with incredulity Wilson's explanation to Congress as he asked for a declaration of war, that America had 'no quarrel with the German people.'

Conditions bettered at the camp, men were allowed to walk outside of its confines . . . until Fikentscher escaped from Malta in a boat. Security was tightened again, privileges were taken away.

Von Müller, with little warning, was removed to England.

Meanwhile, von Muecke and the remnants of his Direction Island raiding party were miraculously back in Germany, and some of them engaged once more in prosecuting the war. Their saga read like fantasy:

. . . from Direction Island, *Ayesha*, flying the German

ensign, had sailed due north to the Dutch port of Padang, Sumatra. There von Muecke's fortuitous mixture of charm and arrogance convinced the authorities that the *Ayesha* should be reprovisioned and not interned as an enemy warship. This bespoke genius since von Muecke had to declare *Ayesha* a fighting craft of the Imperial German Navy or else admit having pirated her in the first place.

Ayesha was manned like no other 'warship' afloat. For one thing, her slow speed offered little relief from the tropical heat. The crew sat in the rigging or lay under canvas awnings completely nude. The craft and her crew materialized out of the mist one day in the Indian Ocean in front of the 1,700-ton Lloyd steamer *Choising*, and gave the latter's crew quite a shock.

The *Choising* had originally been assigned as a collier for the *Emden* but had never reached her. Von Muecke now took over the larger vessel and scuttled the *Ayesha*. He had various plans of operation: join up with the *Königsberg* (which he could not have known was already neutralized in the Rufiji River, East Africa) or even make contact with his country's troops fighting in South-east Africa.

Finally, with a new name—*Shenir*, Genoa—painted on her stern, the *Choising* cruised northward and west in the Indian Ocean until she was ploughing through the narrow waters of the Red Sea, thick with the warships of the English and most of the other navies which were enemy to Germany. She arrived at the Arabian port of Hodeida, above the Straits of Bab el Mandeb, at the southern approaches to the Sea. Von Muecke learned that it was in the hands of the Turks.

Then began a long journey across the desert on mules and donkeys, finally ending at a place called Sana. Here the men despaired of going further overland and returned to Hodeida, where the *Emden*'s sailors once more tried to beat their way home by sea, this time in two native dhows. One was soon wrecked on a reef, and its passengers were transferred to the remaining craft.

Only through von Muecke's excellent seamanship and indomitable spirit did he survive the nightly 'louse hunts' and depleted food supplies to bring his men safely to the port of Leet. There he lost his first man— to typhus.

Now they pushed across the desert again, by camel, in the general direction of Constantinople. Von Muecke had watched over his supply of pistols, rifles and machine guns with a mother hen's zeal, even to diving for those which had been submerged in the sunken dhow. He was to need them in his desert journey.

For three days, von Muecke and his men, together with their Arab guards were kept under attack by a desert tribe of Bedouins, fighting Indian fashion behind sand dunes, rocks and any indenture or rise in the Arabian wasteland which could afford cover. Against superior numbers, the Germans defended themselves valiantly, losing six of their company and claiming at least three times as many casualties among the bandits.

When at last von Müller's first officer brought his bronzed, ragged and weary group to Haidar Pasha, across the Bosphorus from Constantinople, he was able to announce to the senior Turkish naval officer in command:

'I report the landing squad from the *Emden*, five officers, seven petty officers and thirty men strong.'

Von Müller's arrival in Rotterdam from England, one chilly, damp morning after the Armistice was less spectacular. He looked older, drawn and gaunt. His sister Elfreda was at the station to meet him.

There could be no joy in the heart of the *Emden*'s captain. He had returned to a land bowed in defeat. There were not the physical ravages that the people of Belgium and France knew, but his homeland was nonetheless hushed and sullen under a subjugation which was real.

Sorrow had visited almost every home. Germany counted more than seven million casualties. The effectiveness of an entire generation—the youthful and all-important one—was gone.

Deflation had started to gnaw at the economic life of the nation and of its individual citizens. The blockade, which the U-boats with all their early successes had been unable to break, had contributed to the collapse of the mark as well as to the more obvious matters of food supply. Lean faces, young and old, were to be seen on every German street.

To von Müller it seemed as though a song had been silenced throughout his country, as though in a bright, gay room the lights had suddenly been switched off.

He returned to Blankenburg, like one who cannot awake from a bad dream, who is in familiar surroundings which nonetheless aren't *quite* the same. He believed he should be able to reach out and bring back the world of yesterday . . . but he could not make that effort, no more than could anyone else.

In the night he listened to the town's noises he had known five years before; the petulant whistles of the trains . . . yet, he knew the freighters must be half-empty, when no one had money to buy goods, and the passenger coaches were carrying not peacetime travellers, but the wounded, the shocked, the imbecilic back home.

Constant and undiminished only were stairway creakings, tap drip-drippings, and from somewhere near the cry and gurgle as a baby turned in sleep.

In the morning, von Müller would be up early to walk the streets, restlessly, wondering what to do . . . for what was there for a professional naval officer in a defeated nation to do? The smoky haze of a town at dawn would be mantling iridescently the gables and chimney tops. The rooks would be cawing overhead as they foraged and from those windows where there was still a variety of food would filter the aroma of breakfast, the cry of children about to burst from their bondage of night and masonry . . . these were familiar manifestations of the coming-awake city.

But they held scant comfort for Karl von Müller.

Even in the beer halls they sang,

> *Deutschland, Deutschland über alles,*
> *Über alles in der Welt . . . !*

. . . as though it were a requiem. Indeed, von Müller had reason to believe it was.

Soon in Hanover, in central Germany, where old gabled buildings of medieval times managed to exist next to the shapes of modern industry, he married Jutta von Hanstein.

He was to prove, unfortunately, no exception to a pattern that history had established for warriors in the wake of wars.

To the much more encompassing civilian world, military leaders who rise out of nowhere to fill the exacting needs of wartime appear at once extraordinary and ephemeral creatures. Those who do not perish, perhaps mercifully, in the holocaust which spawned them are faced with a challenge to adapt to civilian living. They tend to become anachronisms in a peacetime world, by society's harsh standards.

Many factors conspired to drive deeper the hurts in von Müller's soul, especially the Bolshevist revolution within his beloved Navy. The national spectre of unemployment showed no favouritism to war heroes.

Von Müller, however, was elected to the Brunswick Diet, a job which kept him, his wife and infant daughter Elfreda from much of the hunger which gnawed at the souls of his countrymen. He also drew his Navy pension.

He wrote spasmodically on a manuscript which was to be the biography of his life. But, somehow, the man who could organize and execute naval missions with brilliance and courage could not follow it through to a successful climax.

Late at night he could be seen in the parlour of his home, a man far older than his years, his brow deepening with lines. He would sit, over a book, or his manuscript, smoking, thinking. . . .

What Thomas Gray had penned almost two centuries before was still relevant:

He gave to Mis'ry all he had, a tear,
He gained from Heav'n ('twas all he wished)
a friend.

The years moved slowly on. The Atlantic was
spanned by air, the Treaty of Versailles was signed.
The League of Nations was born. The Weimar Republic
proved to have less effective leadership over its country
than did the Kaiser.

German shopkeepers posed with wheelbarrows full of
deflated marks, and across the Atlantic, newspaper
readers were disposed to chuckle. After all, 1929 was
still several years off for America.

On January 20th, 1923, his second daughter Karla was
born. Two weeks later, on a trip to Brunswick to
attend a meeting of the Diet he contracted a severe
cold. Pneumonia and then pleurisy set in.

The doctor quarantined his newborn, as well as Karla
and little Elfreda, now a year and a half old, in another
house. His sister helped nurse him.

But Karl von Müller's heart was not up to the strain.
On March 11th, the Captain of the *Emden* died. He
was 50.

His passing was attended by a serenity far from
symbolic of his destiny in the waking realm of being.

On the other hand, for quite a different breed of
German the world was just beginning. The very day
after von Müller's funeral, a rabble-rouser, shell-shocked
veteran of the Western Front, who had assumed the
name Adolf Hitler, launched a beer hall *putsch* in Munich.
It was unsuccessful, but others would follow which
would be far from abortive.

To-day there is little to remind one that a lonely, thoughtful and uncommonly noble man had ever walked the face of this earth. In Blankenburg one exception is in the form of a bronze bust of its naval-officer citizen, on a strip of greensward, opposite the Stadthaus. It is close enough to the Harz Mountains so that the sighing of many trees can be heard at night, as a whisper. But the sea and all it meant in the existence of Karl von Müller is little more than a dream to the city's inhabitants, and a splash of colour in travel posters.

Far from Blankenburg, in scattered other hamlets are a fast dwindling band who do remember and in whose hearts still rings the song which forty-two long years ago they themselves helped to pen, impassioned, imperishable:

> Ship without harbour, ship without rest,
> Our flying *Emden*, we love thee best
> Singing thy deeds in German verse
> Ever behind thee, the English curse,
> Ship after ship sent down to the deep
> But the sea, the broad sea, was thine to keep.
>
> Ship without harbour, ship without rest
> Wonderful *Emden*, we love thee best
> Even though struck by the enemy shell
> Even though burned by a raging hell
> Even though sunk on a far away shore
> Hast been forgotten? No, nevermore,
>   nevermore . . . !

INDEX

LONELY COMMAND
The Epic Story of the *Emden*

by

A. A. HOEHLING

No fighting vessel of World War I achieved the almost legendary fame and acclaim of the German cruiser *Emden*. This book tells the story of the *Emden,* of her captain, Karl Von Müller, and of her crew who bravely faced the perils of war as they sailed and fought on a ship to which they were, every man of them, devoted beyond the call of duty.

One of the epic tales of the sea, this documentary account of the *Emden* is not only a thrilling adventure but also an incisive examination of the "loneliness of heart and soul which only those who have known command, and command by themselves, can fully understand."

Under Captain Von Müller, a man of brilliance and daring, the *Emden* became the terror of the Indian Ocean as a lone raider that left a trail of sunken ships behind her. During the first three months of World War I, she destroyed a hundred thousand tons of Allied ship-